Approaching
EASTER

In grateful thanks for the life of
Geoffrey Paul, my father

Approaching EASTER

JANE WILLIAMS

LION

Copyright © 2006 Jane Williams
This edition copyright © 2006 Lion Hudson

The author asserts the moral right
to be identified as the author of this work

A Lion Book
an imprint of
Lion Hudson plc
Mayfield House, 256 Banbury Road,
Oxford OX2 7DH, England
www.lionhudson.com
ISBN-13: 978-0-7459-5199-7
ISBN-10: 0-7459-5199-6

First edition 2006
10 9 8 7 6 5 4 3 2 1 0

A catalogue record for this book is available
from the British Library

Typeset in 12/16 Lapidary333
Printed and bound in China

Contents

Preface

When my father died, we found on his desk the beginning of a sermon that he was preparing to give about Jesus' resurrection from the dead. The calm certainty of the way he started what he was going to say was both a comfort and a challenge to us who were left behind. We were glad to know that he faced his own death with no fear, but we missed him; for us, Jesus' promise that one day we too shall rise from the dead seemed, at that moment, a poor exchange for the presence of a much-loved husband and father.

The themes of Lent, Holy Week and Easter are hugely important, and not just to Christians. Lent is a time for thinking about what controls us, what gives meaning to our lives, while Holy Week and Easter make us focus on the great themes of life and death.

The history of how and why Jesus died on the cross is at least partly an analysis of what we all do to one another when we are controlled by fear, or greed, or love of power, or too much love of ourselves. At every turn, Jesus challenges us to be brave enough to step out of our self-made prisons and turn towards the source of life and freedom, which he calls God. Unfortunately, too many of us don't see fear, greed, love of power and love of ourselves as prisons. We see these emotions as necessary to grab what we think we need for our own security; we might even be prepared to kill for them, just as people 2,000 years ago were prepared to kill Jesus rather than to hear his challenge.

Jesus taught that the only life worth having is a life shared with others, a life that brings challenging freedom to everyone. A selfish life, turned in on itself, and concerned only with self-protection, is already too much like death to be worth bothering with. Jesus' teaching is something that many, many people, of all faiths or none, believe and live out in the generosity of their daily lives. Believers see this as beginning to share in God's own self-giving life, and are often humbled by the way that others, who don't use that language, will still live it out.

Easter is the great celebration of life. It is not an attempt to deny the reality of death, but simply to say that we don't live to die. We live to share and make life possible for others. Christians believe that God's life is shared so powerfully and with such love that nothing can end what God gives us. Even beyond our death, God still has more to give and to share.

The longing to give life, and to do everything we can to make sure that the lives that come after ours will not suffer because of the choices we have made, is what drives our thoughts in the weeks before Easter, whether we naturally put God at the heart of our actions or not.

It is now nearly a quarter of a century since my father died, and I still miss him. I take great comfort from having met so many people who were enriched by knowing him, and they have all helped me to see something of the meaning of Easter. My dear dad obviously helped a lot of people to believe in life, partly through his own understanding of the resurrection. I dedicate this book to his memory.

T hen Jesus was led up by the Spirit into the wilderness to be tempted by the devil. He fasted for forty days and forty nights, and afterwards he was famished. The tempter came and said to him, 'If you are the Son of God, command these stones to become loaves of bread.' But he answered, 'It is written, "One does not live by bread alone, but by every word that comes from the mouth of God." '

Then the devil took him to the holy city and placed him on the pinnacle of the temple, saying to him, 'If you are the Son of God, throw yourself down; for it is written, "He will command his angels concerning you", and "On their hands they will bear you up, so that you will not dash your foot against a stone." '

Jesus said to him, 'Again it is written, "Do not put the Lord your God to the test." '

Again, the devil took him to a very high mountain and showed him all the kingdoms of the world and their splendour; and he said to him, 'All these I will give you, if you will fall down and worship me.' Jesus said to him, 'Away with you, Satan! For it is written, "Worship the Lord your God and serve only him." '

Then the devil left him, and suddenly angels came and waited on him.   MATTHEW 4:1–11

CHAPTER 1

Forty Days

Do you remember when you were a small child how long a day could seem? When you got home from school, and your mother asked you what you had had for school dinners, you genuinely couldn't remember, because it seemed such a long time ago! In reality, of course, it was only two or three hours, but when you are young it seems like an eternity. Sadly, as you grow older time no longer seems to operate in this way. I've now turned into one of those annoying adults who say to teenage acquaintances, 'My, how you've grown! I remember when you were just a baby!' However, there are still passages of time that creep as slowly as they did when we were children, and seem to take disproportionate amounts of space. Pain or boredom or worry, in particular, are good examples of this.

The forty days of Lent, starting from Ash Wednesday, are not supposed to be full of pain or worry (though I personally think that a bit of boredom is good for people from time to time!), but they *are* supposed to feel like a long time. Lent is supposed to feel long enough for you really to experience something, and to remember it afterwards. Most of us can give up coffee or alcohol or chocolate for a day or two without really noticing, but to give them up for forty days is quite another matter. Your body will really notice that you have taken away something that it was used to receiving on a regular basis. It will make you feel that loss. Gradually, as the days go by, though, your body will not remember its need for that particular fix any more. You will have changed something. Forty days is long enough to change all but the most deeply rooted habits.

That's not the reason why Lent lasts for forty days, but it is a helpful piece of coincidence. The real reason is that forty days is the period of time that Jesus spent in the wilderness, as we read in Matthew's Gospel. We keep Lent to try to share some of that experience with him.

We usually think of Lent in negative terms. If we keep it at all, we keep it by 'giving things up'. I've already made that assumption in what I've just said. The most usual things to give up are the things that we know in our heart of hearts are bad for us, so that Lent becomes a means of killing two birds with one stone. We have the satisfaction of improving our health *and* feeling pious. What could be better?

Now John wore clothing of camel's hair with a leather belt around his waist, and his food was locusts and wild honey. Then the people of Jerusalem and all Judea were going out to him, and all the region along the Jordan, and they were

baptized by him in the river Jordan, confessing their sins.

But when he saw many Pharisees and Sadducees coming for baptism, he said to them, 'You brood of vipers! Who warned you to flee from the wrath to come? ... I baptize you with water for repentance, but one who is more powerful than I is coming after me; I am not worthy to carry his sandals. He will baptize you with the Holy Spirit and fire'...

Then Jesus came from Galilee to John at the Jordan, to be baptized by him. John would have prevented him, saying, 'I need to be baptized by you, and do you come to me?' But Jesus answered him, 'Let it be so now; for it is proper for us in this way to fulfil all righteousness.' Then he consented. And when Jesus had been baptized, just as he came up from the water, suddenly the heavens were opened to him and he saw the Spirit of God descending like a dove and alighting on him. And a voice from heaven said, 'This is my Son, the Beloved, with whom I am well pleased.'

Then Jesus was led up by the Spirit into the wilderness to be tempted by the devil.

MATTHEW 3:4–7, 13–17; 4:1

But, interestingly, that is not how Lent starts. As we discover in the Bible, Jesus went into the wilderness not to give something up, but to discover the meaning of something he had just been given. What we celebrate as Lent is the start of Jesus' ministry. Immediately before he goes into the desert, Jesus is baptized in the River Jordan by John the Baptist. John is a very Lenten figure. He wears animal skins, and is reputed to have had a strict organic diet. He lives, we are told, on locusts and honey, so I think we can safely assume that he was not on the plump side. He preaches hell-fire and damnation, and he is not afraid to tell the rich and the religious exactly what he thinks of them. He calls the Pharisees and Sadducees – senior religious leaders – 'vipers', and says, 'Who warned you to flee from the wrath to come?' (Matthew 3:7).

People just love John and his style of preaching, and they go out to the river in their droves to hear him preach and to repent and try to change their ways. They go very much in the spirit in which we now approach Lent. They slightly doubt if their attempt is going to last long, but they are willing to try. No doubt some of John's followers made a lifelong commitment, but for many people he was just the latest religious craze.

Jesus, the younger man, the up-and-coming guru who is very likely to be the next craze, goes along to the River Jordan, too. The Gospel stories don't tell us why, but we can imagine that it is partly out of a desire to show respect to John, and to give credit to what John has been doing. Jesus has no wish to set up in rivalry with John, and he wants everyone to see that.

The Christmas story tells us that John and Jesus have already met, though not exactly face to face. Their pregnant mothers supported each other and John, growing in his mother's womb, recognized Jesus as divine and danced for joy. We have no idea at all if they met between that moment and this turning point at the

river, when both are adults, but John recognizes Jesus, not as someone he's met many times before, but more like someone he has seen in his dreams. John instantly realizes that his own ministry is over, and that it is time to hand over to Jesus. He says, 'I need to be baptized by you, and do you come to me?' (Matthew 3:14).

If this is a hard realization, he gives no indication of it in his gracious words of welcome and acclamation for Jesus. And considering that the riverbank is crowded with people who have come out from all the local towns and villages specifically to see John, not Jesus, I think it says a great deal about John. He is still at the height of his powers, but he instantly concedes to Jesus. He has always known that his work is not about himself, and that he is only supposed to be the warm-up act. He has always described himself as just the herald, announcing the coming of the really important person. But I wonder how many of us would have been able to keep focused on that, with the kind of popular acclaim John was receiving. Was he really never tempted to wonder if perhaps he was to be the real thing after all, and not just the forerunner?

There is a story that I was very fond of as a child. It is called *The Dean's Watch*, by Elizabeth Goudge, and it's about the people who live in a great cathedral city, one of whom is a watchmaker called Isaac. Isaac is brilliant at his job, and he knows it – not with arrogance, but with simple certainty. However, he meets a boy called Job, whom he quickly realizes is going to be even better.

He was a finer craftsman even than Isaac, and he knew it, and so, presently, did Isaac. There was a greatness in Isaac. One evening at supper, between one bit of sausage and another, he was able to acknowledge that it was so. 'He must increase, but I must decrease,' he said to himself. He did not know where the quotation came from, or that in applying it to himself he had taken a fence at which many baulked or fell. He finished the sausage without having the slightest idea that he was not the same man that he had been when he embarked upon it.

Isaac has no idea that being willing to be diminished so that Job can grow is a sign of greatness. But it *is*, just as it was for John the Baptist. Now, as John sees Jesus, he knows at once that he has to stand back. Everything he has done has been in preparation for this moment, when he would see Jesus and know him. He had said, 'I baptize you with water for repentance, but one who is more powerful than I is coming after me. I am not worthy to carry his sandals' (Matthew 3:11). Now his prophecy is coming true, and he is face to face with the man who is to take over.

Imagine what that felt like for Jesus. Here he is, part of the noisy, pushing crowd, all waiting to be told their sins by John and be baptized in the river by him, and suddenly the whole picture freezes as John sees him. It is as though everyone else has vanished, and they are alone, with the river behind them providing the watery noises of the amniotic fluids in which they first met.

The Gospels, tantalizingly, almost never tell us what Jesus is thinking and feeling, because they are all about how other people react to him, rather than about Jesus' own inner life. But it is perfectly clear that this moment at the river is a turning point, and that John's generous recognition is part of what allows Jesus to go forward. It is the moment when the whole course of Jesus' life is decided. From now on, Jesus is set on the course of preaching and teaching that is to lead inexorably to his death.

We don't know how Jesus would have described himself

before this moment, or what he would have said God was asking him to do, but from this moment on, his life and work and words are characterized by the enormous authority of one who knows he is doing God's will.

John does not want to baptize Jesus. He has been baptizing people as a symbol of their repentance, but he knows that Jesus is going to do exactly what God wants him to, and so really doesn't need to repent. John is ready to give up his own work straight away and hand over to Jesus. But Jesus insists. He takes John's characteristic practice – baptism – and makes it something new. Jesus goes down into the water as into the grave, but also as into his mother's womb again. He accepts both his own death and his new life as he allows John to immerse him in the water.

But if John's words of acceptance and praise are important, what happens next is even more important. As Jesus comes up out of the water, God confirms John's recognition with the dove, who represents the Holy Spirit, resting on Jesus' head, and the words of acceptance that God says. 'Yes,' God says, 'this is the one. You are my beloved Son. Everything you are and everything you do gives me joy.' Most children long to hear something like that from their parents. In the weary, painful and terrifying months that followed, how often Jesus must have needed to repeat God's words to himself.

It is important to remember that Jesus' work is grounded in this sense of knowing who he is, and knowing he is loved. He has the human witness of John, as well as God's own voice ringing in his ears. He does need both, so that he can know he has not deceived himself. But it is out of this strong sense of self-worth that Jesus' ministry is born. Too much of what we do is driven by insecurity or self-loathing, and by our desire to please people and win their approval. It is as though here, at the River Jordan, at the start of Jesus' public life, God is modelling just what we all

need if we are to do what we have to. We need to know that we are loved and trusted. Without that knowledge, we will always be acting out of a false sense of ourselves, not out of the central reality of our being. It is because Jesus knows who he is and how much God loves him that he can do what has to be done.

That doesn't mean that it is going to be easy. When Jesus has heard God's voice, and seen the dove, and accepted John's recognition, that is when he has to go off into the desert alone, for forty days. He needs time to come to terms with the enormity of being loved and trusted. Being loved and trusted by someone carries huge responsibilities with it for any one of us. But to be loved and trusted by God, as Jesus is, is really sobering.

So what we set ourselves to do in Lent has several different aspects. First, there is John's part. We need to learn to see the value of others, which will sometimes mean being prepared to take a back seat ourselves. Our satisfaction will come from knowing we are doing what we were born for, and that our words of encouragement to someone else at the right moment may allow them to fulfil their promise, too. That will not necessarily be an easy thing for us to do. So the forty days of Lent may profitably be used to get to know ourselves again. What are we good at? What should we be letting go of? How can we genuinely assess what we were put on this earth for?

Then we need to pause and give thanks to all of those who have done John's job for us. It is hard to make time regularly to take stock of everyone who has helped us on our way, and given us the words of praise that we needed when we were not sure of ourselves. Lent might be a good time to remember them.

Finally, Lent is a time to hear and try to believe that God loves us, and then to spend at least the forty days attempting to find out what that means. At the heart of the Christian story is the belief that God made the world and everything in it out of love. Jesus came to live and die for us so that we can understand God's words to him as being meant for us, too: 'You are my beloved daughters and sons; you give me pleasure.' Being loved by God has implications for how we then live our lives in that knowledge. However, there are many things that distract us both from knowing how much we are valued and from thinking through what that means. When Jesus hears God's words, he sets out to a place of quiet and solitude – the desert – so that he can think and pray about them. That isn't an option for most of us, but perhaps we can make a little time in the forty days of Lent to try to think about what our lives are for. And that might mean giving up, at least for a bit, some of the things that distract us, so that we can focus better on the essentials. 'Giving things up' does come in at last, but perhaps not for the reasons that we initially thought.

In *A Season for the Spirit*, Martin Smith writes,

Lent is about freedom which is gained only through exposure to the truth… Truth is not a thing, it is rather an event. Truth happens to us when the coverings of illusion are stripped away and what is real emerges into the open... The Spirit promises to bring us into truth by stripping away some more of the insulation and barriers which have separated us from living contact with reality, the reality of God, of God's world, and our true selves.

CHAPTER 2

Food

Like many other young people, I had anorexia as a teenager. I was not as seriously ill as others I have known, and I didn't have to be hospitalized, but the effect on my personality was quite dramatic, for a bit. All such life-changing experiences, good and bad, make us want to ask, 'What if? What if it hadn't happened? How different would I be?' In the end, these are unanswerable and futile questions, but I am still intrigued at the power of such an illness. After all, it is really only about what you do and don't eat, isn't it?

But, of course, there is no 'only' about it. Food is an immensely powerful symbol of personality, of power, of circumstances, of feeling. 'You are what you eat,' we say. I don't think we mean exactly that. We cannot make ourselves intelligent or funny or kind through what we eat, although some people would argue that we can improve or diminish our natural talents in those areas through our food choices. 'You are what you eat' says exactly that – that we have choices we can freely make, about our lives and our health. In other words, our eating habits are partly about control of our environment. That may be why we get so very anxious about food scares. Whenever some commonly used food substance is said to be cancer-producing, for example, supermarkets and food advisers are inundated with queries from terrified customers. I am not in any way suggesting that that is wrong, but I do find it interesting that we are prepared to tolerate all kinds of other environmental things that we know cause bad health – such as cars, for example. But something about the intimacy of food, the fact that we knowingly and voluntarily put it into our bodies, makes it feel like a different kind of choice.

Certainly in my case, anorexia was about choice and control. Although it started off as simply a diet embarked on by a plump teenage girl, I quickly discovered the power that refusing to eat gave me. For one thing, it worried my parents and the other adults who were supposed to be taking care of me. Being able to feed your young is one of the most basic of urges, and I was denying them. Also, in a boarding school where very little of daily life was under my control, this felt like one area of autonomy. Nobody could make me eat, at least. Subconsciously, I think I was also making choices about sexuality. It was a girls-only school, with a highly charged atmosphere that required a lot of gossip about boys and make-up and clothes; I think I was choosing, probably rather priggishly, to have nothing to do with all that. But the result of all those free and powerful choices was that I made myself ill, and lost all control of the weapon I thought I had chosen to control others. I could no longer eat, even if I wanted to.

Given the power of our relationship with food, it is hardly surprising that most religious traditions take food very seriously. Holy days are often simply called 'feast days', and the most sacred times always have special food associated with them. In Britain, for example, we make hot cross buns for Good Friday and simnel cake for Easter Day. Other cultures have their own versions of these, and there are many delicacies baked around the world for Christmas.

To balance the festive enjoyment of food, religious observance also requires abstinence at other times. Muslims fast from sun up

to sunset during Ramadan, and Christians are encouraged to give up rich food and alcohol during Lent. That's why Lent starts with Shrove Tuesday, or Mardi Gras, where we use up all our forbidden foods in one big burst of fun, before entering the serious season of fasting and prayer. In England, Shrove Tuesday is sometimes just called 'pancake day'. The theory is that we use up all our eggs and butter and milk, and don't get any more until Easter. In many households, making pancakes has persisted, but it is not necessarily followed by the austerity of Lent.

It may seem as though religious practice is sending out mixed messages about food – one minute encouraging people to gorge and the next minute requiring them to fast – but actually, there is one coherent message coming through: food is so powerful that it needs to be kept in its proper place. It is one of the great joys of life, and it is proper to enjoy it and celebrate it, but it can quickly take over and warp our perspective. Just how badly it can throw lives off balance is shown not only by anorexics like my teenage self, but also by the whole shocking contrast between the growing obesity crisis in the West and the growing number of deaths from starvation in the Third World. Clearly, ours is not a world that knows how to keep food in balance. We desperately need to know how to celebrate food without allowing it to control us. It is as though we are frightened of our own urges and don't know how to cope with them, except by indulging them or punishing them. Learning to be at home with food cannot be achieved until we learn to know and trust ourselves, and so to put food in its proper context. One of my favourite recipe books (Nigella Lawson's *How to Eat*) puts this very succinctly in its preface:

> *Cooking is not about just joining the dots, following one recipe slavishly and then moving on to the next. It's about developing an understanding of food, a sense of assurance in the kitchen, about the simple desire to make yourself something to eat. And in cooking, as in writing, you must please yourself to please others. Strangely it can take enormous confidence to trust your own palate, follow your own instincts. Without habit, which itself is just trial and error, this can be harder than following the most elaborate of recipes. But it's what works, what's important.*

During Lent, it is particularly illuminating to contemplate that interplay between confidence and habit. So many of our habits are born out of lack of confidence, but we could choose to spend the forty days of Lent building habits based on our strengths. In relating to food, that could mean giving up unrealistic expectations of weight loss, and learning to hear our bodies again. They probably need neither as much nor as little food as we sometimes assume.

In this context, it is fascinating to note that food is the first temptation that Jesus faces when he is out in the desert, coming to terms with God's call on his life. We are told that he has fasted for days, and in his weakened and hallucinatory state, all his deepest needs are articulated for him as temptations. The

temptations come as an offer to him of all the things he most
wants and needs, starting with the most pressing, which is food.

The tempter does not come to Jesus armed with a picnic
basket full of goodies to waft under his famished nose. Nothing
so straightforward. Instead, he suggests that Jesus should use his
God-given powers to make food for himself. 'Turn the stones into
bread,' the insidious voice suggests. Other stories in the Gospels
suggest that Jesus is more than capable of doing that. There is,
for example, the story of the day when a huge crowd of people
has followed Jesus for miles, and as evening approaches they are

all far from home and very hungry. Jesus looks around and spots a boy who has had the foresight to bring himself a packed lunch of bread and fish. Jesus takes it, prays over it and makes from that one small basket of food enough to feed the whole crowd of thousands.

After this Jesus went to the other side of the Sea of Galilee, also called the Sea of Tiberias. A large crowd kept following him, because they saw the signs that he was doing for the sick. Jesus went up the mountain and sat down there with his disciples. Now the Passover, the festival of the Jews, was near. When he looked up and saw a large crowd coming towards him, Jesus said to Philip, 'Where are we to buy bread for these people to eat?' He said this to test him, for he himself knew what he was going to do. Philip answered him, 'Six months' wages would not buy enough bread for each of them to get a little.' One of his disciples, Andrew, Simon Peter's brother, said to him, 'There is a boy here who has five barley loaves and two fish. But what are they, among so many people?' Jesus said, 'Make the people sit down.' Now there was a great deal of grass in the place; so they sat down, about five thousand in all. Then Jesus took the loaves, and when he had given thanks, he distributed them to

those who were seated; so also the fish, as much as
they wanted. When they were satisfied, he told his
disciples, 'Gather up the fragments left over, so that
nothing may be lost.' So they gathered them up,
and from the fragments of the five barley loaves,
left by those who had eaten, they filled twelve
baskets. When the people saw the sign that he had
done, they began to say, 'This is indeed the prophet
who is to come into the world.'

JOHN 6:1–14

There really isn't any doubt that Jesus could have turned the
stones into bread. It's hard to see what harm there can be in
such a suggestion. After all, food is good, and people are designed
to eat it. In the rest of his ministry, Jesus seems to be the kind of
person who enjoys a good party. He is always getting into trouble
with religious people for agreeing to eat with the wrong kind of
people. Jesus had no qualms about breaking all kinds of food
taboos, such as picking grain to eat on the sabbath, which was
forbidden by the religious experts of the Judaism of his day. It's
not as though Jesus is contemplating conjuring himself up a feast
of caviar and champagne; just bread, the basic staple of life. Nor
is there anyone else around. Out in the desert, miles from
anywhere, Jesus could do it without showing off.

So it is not so much food as such that Jesus is rejecting, but the notion that food should have a disproportionate place in life. Later on in his ministry, Jesus says that God is like a good father, who would never dream of giving his children stones when they asked for bread, or snakes when they asked for fish. God knows what is good for us, and what is bad.

'Ask, and it will be given to you; search, and you will find; knock, and the door will be opened for you. For everyone who asks receives, and everyone who searches finds, and for everyone who knocks, the door will be opened. Is there anyone among you who, if your child asks for bread, will give a stone? Or if the child asks for a fish, will give a snake? If you then, who are evil, know how to give good gifts to your children, how much more will your Father in heaven give good things to those who ask him!'

MATTHEW 7:7–11

I wonder if, as Jesus talks about God feeding his people, he remembers that day in the desert when he himself preferred stones to bread that had not been given him by God? Because that is the choice Jesus makes, here in the desert. He makes the choice about what will be central in his life. Bread is not the most important thing in life, he discovers. Even though he is

starving, he will not let his hunger define him. He chooses
instead to be defined in relation to God. The voice at his baptism
has told him so, and he chooses, now, alone and hungry in the
desert, still to be only God's child. He will not be a victim,

someone driven by his own desperate needs, someone with no choices. He will choose instead to be the beloved child of God.

Giving up something for Lent might feel like self-denial, but it is actually a way of finding ourselves. What defines us, most essentially? Is it our weaknesses or our strengths? If we choose to give up something that we thought we needed, or that we like so much that we thought it was part of our nature, we might be pleasantly surprised to find that, without it, we are still ourselves. So we will not, after all, fall apart without coffee or chocolate or a glass of wine. We are stronger than that, freer than that.

If we could really begin to believe in our freedom, then we could enjoy food for the pleasure that it is, and remember that that is all it is. Perhaps we might also begin to be able to share our food with others. There are, after all, so many people in the world who do not have the luxury of giving things up for Lent, because they have nothing to give up. They cannot discover their freedom and strength because they are genuinely starving. Lent helps us to discover that we do not really need nearly as much as we thought we did in order to be the people we are capable of being. So now we can be generous and see the needs of others. If we are no longer afraid that we are dependent upon our luxuries, perhaps we will be brave enough to give them up so that others can have what they need.

I end this section with a poem by Robert Herrick, entitled 'To Keep a True Lent'.

Is this a Fast, to keep
The Larder lean
And clean
From fat of veals and sheep?…

No; 'tis a Fast, to dole
Thy sheaf of wheat
And meat
Unto the hungry soul…

To show a heart grief-rent;
To starve thy sin,
Not bin,
And that's to keep thy Lent.

CHAPTER 3

Power

When I was a child, my sisters and I had all kinds of crazes. One of the most virulent was for plastic trolls. They came in several different sizes, from just a few inches high to nearly the size of a human baby. They were not at all pretty – quite the contrary, in fact – but they had long, flowing hair, which we imagined gave clues to their names and characters. So the troll with purple hair was called Plum and was a warm, home-loving body, while the one with orange hair was called Flame, and was wild and unpredictable. We saved up our pocket money for them avidly, and traded them with merciless determination. Because I was a thrifty child (a characteristic that I seem, sadly, to have lost in later life), I was often in a position to acquire trolls from more indigent sisters, and so soon built up quite a collection.

The interesting thing about this craze, as with so many childhood fads, is that the competition was the whole point of the exercise. The trolls themselves were neither valuable nor interesting nor charming. Their allure lay in the fact that they were desired by others, and so possessing them gave me power. Well, it didn't actually, since being a troll-owner did not in fact enable me to do or be anything that I wasn't already, but because I was envied, I felt powerful.

Power often is quite illusory, it seems. If you ask some of those people we all think of as powerful figures – such as politicians or monarchs – if they feel that they have power, they generally answer no. They feel that their status brings with it so many constraints that they have little freedom to exercise the power for which they are so envied. They may still, of course, have a great deal more freedom and ability to influence events than most of us, but not to the extent that we fantasize about.

The longing for power is not necessarily bad. We might want to have the power to change things for the better, to improve the lives of others, as well as our own. We might even be convinced that we, unlike others, know that with power comes responsibility. But it is interesting to note the deep-seated suspicion of power, and not just in the Christian tradition. 'Absolute power corrupts absolutely,' it is said. Behind that lies the assumption that power is bad for people, and the more power they have, the worse it is. Moreover, it is bad not just for the person who possesses it, but also for their dependants. To feel that someone else is wholly responsible for your life is to remain in perpetual childhood; if we resent this, we remain in a permanent state of discontent, longing for freedom and envying the person who seems to us to have it.

Shakespeare explores this complex dynamic of power and envy in many of his plays. Think, for example, of Othello, the great, charismatic military leader who is turned into a murderer by jealousy.

Othello has won power through his military skill, and he has won himself a beautiful wife (Desdemona), partly through the aura of authority that his success gives him, and partly because he is exotic, from another race and culture, and his stories fascinate her. He should be invulnerable, but Iago, one of his soldiers, hates him for his success, and his hatred gives him the insight that jealousy is the one weapon that will bring Othello down.

The jealousy is firstly Iago's and, because he knows something of the force of its deadly infection, he makes Othello jealous, too.

> For that I do suspect the lusty Moor
> Hath leap'd into my seat: the thought whereof
> Doth like a poisonous mineral gnaw my inwards;
> And nothing can or shall content my soul
> Till I am even'd with him, wife for wife;
> Or failing so, yet that I put the Moor
> At least into a jealousy so strong
> That judgment cannot cure.

Iago does not really care whether or not Othello has had an affair with his wife. He is simply using it as a means to justify the strength of the emotion he feels against Othello. He pulls his jealous anger around him like a comforter, and revels in the strength it gives him. He is a frightening character, wholly controlled by envy and hatred.

He sees Othello's public and private successes and hates him. He sees, too, that although Othello is very successful, he is not really at home with his power, and does not truly believe that it is his own character that has brought him success. He very easily believes that his wife, Desdemona, does not love him.

Iago has brilliantly found the weakness in the otherwise powerful Othello, and he exploits it to bring the man he envies to his knees. Nobody gains from this. Iago will not be promoted into Othello's place; he will simply be faced with another leader to hate. Othello will lose everything that his bravery has won for him – which, ironically, has made him such a figure of hate to Iago. And Desdemona, the faithful and innocent, will lose her life. Perhaps if Othello had been very slightly less successful or Iago very slightly more so, there would have been no story to tell, because although *Othello* is primarily a chilling study of jealousy, it is the distribution of power that gives rise to the jealousy in the first place.

Now while Jesus was at Bethany in the house of Simon the leper, a woman came to him with an alabaster jar of very costly ointment, and she poured it on his head as he sat at the table. But when the disciples saw it, they were angry and said, 'Why this waste? For this ointment could have been sold for a large sum, and the money given to the poor.' But Jesus, aware of this, said to them, 'Why do you trouble the woman? She has performed a good service for me. For you always have the poor with you, but you will not always have me. By pouring this ointment on my body she has prepared me for burial. Truly I tell you, wherever

the good news is proclaimed in the whole world,
what she has done will be told in remembrance of
her.'

Then one of the twelve, who was called Judas
Iscariot, went to the chief priests and said, 'What
will you give me if I betray him to you?' They paid
him thirty pieces of silver. And from that moment
he began to look for an opportunity to betray him.

MATTHEW 26:6–16

Judas is rather like Iago. He is one of Jesus' disciples, a close friend, one of the inner circle, and he suddenly and completely inexplicably turns against Jesus and betrays him.

The Gospel writers give us no clue at all as to Judas's motive. Unlike Shakespeare, the Gospels do not give their characters long monologues that show us their souls. But it is hard not to read Judas's action as part of a power struggle. He sees Jesus, yet again praising someone who can do him no good at all, and he longs to change the situation. He wants Jesus to be one kind of a leader, and Jesus will not do it.

Judas is not the only disciple who tries to push Jesus into a particular course of action. All of them have joined him, at least in part, because they hope that he is going to lead a successful revolution and that they will all benefit from being part of his campaign. They do all have less selfish motives as well, but it is a clear strand in all the Gospels that the disciples hope Jesus is going to be the kind of messiah who will overthrow the oppressive Roman rule and establish an independent Israel with himself at its head, and his faithful followers duly rewarded. The mother of two of his disciples actually comes to Jesus to ask for the best place in the post-revolution government for her sons!

'Declare that these two sons of mine will sit, one at your right hand and one at your left, in your kingdom,' she demands. But Jesus explains to them all, 'You know that the rulers of the Gentiles lord it over them, and their great ones are tyrants over them. It will not be so among you; but whoever wishes to be great among you must be your servant, and whoever wishes to be first among you must be your slave' (Matthew 20:21, 25–27).

Jesus is not interested in that kind of power. He has already made his choice about power, out there in the desert at the beginning of his ministry. Power was one of the temptations that beset him, and he refused. In the desert, he has a vision of a place where there is a wonderful view of the cities and the kingdoms of the world, and all are to be offered to him. All the people in all of those cities will be his followers, and all he has to do is to worship someone who is not God, in exchange for all that power.

It is such an interesting story, with so much left unsaid, so much implied. For one thing, it is not at all clear who could

deliver on the promises made to Jesus. Do all those people in all those cities really answer to someone in such a way? The lure of the temptation relies on the fact that Jesus is semi-starved and weakened and will not think to ask such a question. Just like Iago, the tempter is betraying something about himself in this offer he makes to Jesus. Iago has felt for himself how corrosive jealousy can be, and that's why he knows it will work on Othello. The temptation being offered to Jesus implies that the tempter knows the addictive taste of power, and assumes that Jesus will find it equally strong.

There is no suggestion that, if Jesus falls for the temptation, he will have to use his power over all those lives for evil. Many of us have been tempted to power for the good we believe we can do, and Jesus might equally have felt the same. He knew that he was God's special messenger, and could so easily have persuaded himself that this was the most efficient way to bring many people to worship God. Christian emperors from the centuries after Jesus quite often chose that route, and forcibly Christianized whole populations – for their own good, naturally.

Jesus knows, however, that to accept this power is to allow himself the first steps into the addiction. He rejects that model for himself, and throughout his ministry he rejects it for others, too. Just as he will not be forced, so he will not force others. Those who come to believe in him must do it freely so that, paradoxically, they will win their own freedom through serving Jesus. The will to power can quickly become the master of the person who longs for it, but as Jesus turns away from that, with all its tantalizing promise of personal power and success for himself, he also turns away from the fantasy in which he will be our master. Instead, Jesus chooses to have friends who come to him freely and share the responsibilities, joys and sorrows of his mission in the world.

This choice that Jesus makes in the desert is to influence the whole of his life, and to lead to his death. He chooses never to wield the power he has, as the beloved child of God, to force. He will use it to feed people and heal them, and persuade them, but never to force them, even for their own good. He never offers us the temptation that was offered to him in the desert.

This is how the Bible describes Jesus' temptation: 'Again, the devil took him to a very high mountain and showed him all the kingdoms of the world and their splendour; and he said to him, "All these I will give you, if you will fall down and worship me" ' (Matthew 4:8–9). But Jesus will not accept power at such a cost, and he never promises his followers power in return for worship.

The great irony of it is that, as Jesus turns down the offer to rule over all the kingdoms that he can see; as he turns towards the ministry that is to lead him to the horrible death on the cross; as he chooses to be only what God calls him to be, and never what he could wrest for himself, by his own power; as he does all this he cannot know that over the centuries to come, he will indeed be served and worshipped by people in all of the kingdoms and nations of the world. People will call upon the name of Jesus, not because he is their ruler, with power over them, but because they choose, freely, to believe. 'Conquering Kings their tributes take from the lands they captive make,' the hymn goes. 'Jesus, thine was given thee by the lands thou madest free.'

But Judas can't see that far ahead, either, and he is not happy with the choice that Jesus has made in the desert and continues to make throughout his ministry. He cannot see any sense in it, and he is not alone in that. He can see that Jesus is strong and attractive and full of the power of God, and he believes that Jesus should use his power to bring God's people back to God, by force if necessary, because he knows that will be good for them. He cannot understand why Jesus keeps offering people the choice, and allowing them to reject him.

In the end, Judas cannot stand it any longer, and he makes a plot to hand Jesus over to his enemies. 'What will you give me if I betray him to you?' Judas asks the chief priests (Matthew 26:15). They agree a price of thirty pieces of silver, and the die is cast.

The story does not tell us if Judas kept hoping, right up to the last minute, that this would make Jesus take decisive action. Perhaps he hoped that when Jesus' own safety was threatened, he would at last call his followers to battle and lead the revolution. Or perhaps Judas just wanted to get rid of Jesus. Perhaps he was hoping that he could then take his place, and get on with being the kind of leader that people can understand.

Who knows what Judas hoped? All we do know is that as Jesus was led off to his death, Judas found he could not live with what he had done and so killed himself.

In these stories, Iago and Judas both betray their deepest longings in what they yearn to control. Iago wants to control and destroy Othello, who is everything he could have been, if only he had not been too small a person. Judas is desperate to control Jesus, who has all the power that Judas longs for and yet will not use it as Judas would have done. Perhaps Lent could be a profitable time to review what we long to be in control of, and what price we are prepared to pay to gain that power. As we watch the destructive dynamic of Iago and Othello, Judas and Jesus, we cannot help but be aware that the urge to power puts us in its power. Jesus is the only person in these two scenarios who is free. He has chosen to be only what he is, and to offer that freely, for others to accept or reject. However wonderful the consequences of acceptance might be, Jesus will not force it on us, because he does not want slaves, but friends.

CHAPTER 4

Love

My sisters and I, very typically of teenage girls, were greatly interested in the idea of love. We occasionally bought a magazine that was full of impossibly lovely girls and handsome, square-jawed men, who broke each other's hearts and then mended them again with kisses. Each story finished with a couple locked mouth to mouth and the words 'The End' appearing in a heart-shaped bubble. We knew that that was what that kind of love was supposed to look like.

The stories we used to read about family love were sometimes a bit more challenging, but on the whole, in those dim and distant days, they still assumed that every family had two parents, who were good and caring and protective of the children, unless prevented by war or disaster.

So I remember very vividly the day I discovered Charlotte Brontë's novel, *Jane Eyre*, in our wonderfully welcoming local library. Although I found the book's old-fashioned language rather heavy going, I persisted, initially because of the description of childhood and school days at the beginning of the book. I had recently moved from a boarding school to a day school, and felt a great degree of sympathy for Jane. Even in my most self-pitying moods I could not convince myself that my boarding school had been as bad as Lowood, the dreadful institution to which the orphaned Jane was sent by her unloving relations, but I still felt it gave me a bond with Jane. But as I read on, and reread and reread, it was the relationships that Jane formed that fascinated

me more and more. Not one of them was the kind of 'normal' relationship that I had read about in other books. From her friendship at school with the dying Helen Burns, to her kind but distant affection for Adèle, the little girl to whom the adult Jane goes as a governess, right up to the thrilling but strange relationship she forms with Mr Rochester, her gruff employer, Jane was talking about love in ways that suggested there might be more to it than I had been led to believe.

Jane wasn't pretty or loveable, but she was loyal and intelligent and unusual. Mr Rochester wasn't handsome, but he fizzed with excitement. Jane's family never came to love her, though they did come, very grudgingly, to acknowledge that she had her good points. Little Adèle never became anything but a self-centred, empty-headed little thing, even under the influence of Jane's affection.

But Jane and Mr Rochester spoke of the power of love with extraordinary conviction. Mr Rochester says to Jane, when she is thinking of taking a job far away,

'I sometimes have a queer feeling with regard to you — especially when you are near me, as now; it is as if I had a string somewhere under my left ribs, tightly and inextricably knotted to a similar string situated in the corresponding quarter of your little frame. And if that boisterous channel, and two hundred miles or so of land come broad between us, I am afraid that cord of communion will be snapt; and then I've a nervous notion I should take to bleeding inwardly.'

I know *Jane Eyre* spawned a whole new genre of romance literature, which has its own illusions and conventions, just like any other. But I still think it is a tougher, less sentimental myth than a lot of the modern versions. For one thing, Jane does not allow her love to overrule her morals. When she discovers that Mr Rochester is already married, even though his wife is a violent lunatic and no one could expect Rochester to remain faithful to her, still Jane leaves him. Most modern films of the book cannot make this choice comprehensible, because the modern myth of love is all about sexual fulfilment. Nowadays, people seem to think that to satisfy sexual desire is an overriding imperative, and they are prepared to break up families and sacrifice careers for it. So Jane's choice seems simply cold and harsh.

The drawback with the modern myth about love is that it is all about feelings. Although we are all looking, as Jane was, for something called love, something that will make us feel special, central and all-important to at least one other person, because our myth of love is indistinguishable from sentiment, it has difficulty getting beyond the heart-shaped happy ending. When it gets to that stage of the story, we don't know what to do next, and so we quickly conclude that we are no longer loved. We start to look around for our next fix, our next emotional high, our next feeling of being 'in love'. Many children, born while their parents were 'in love', suffer from this myth, as one or other partner leaves to search for the overriding feeling again.

As far as the Gospels tell us, Jesus did not 'fall in love', but that does not mean that he was not attracted by the myth of being central, being cherished, being special to one other person. After his baptism, Jesus knows that he is God's beloved Son, and he goes away alone to take some time to get used to that fact. To be the beloved Son of God is certainly special. How could he not be tempted to find out just exactly how special?

'What if I were to throw myself down from a very high point?' he muses. 'Would God love me enough to rescue me? God has the power to do that. He could just send an angel or two to catch me and make me float to earth, just like Superman catching Lois Lane, as she falls from a skyscraper.' (Admittedly, that is not the image that would have occurred to Jesus, but it's the one that comes to my mind, as I fictionalize Jesus' temptation!) God is certainly more powerful than any fictional superhero, and Jesus is more central to God's life and God's purposes than any hero's sidekick.

But this picture of God's love is like the romantic myth. It has God as the kind of hero who is prepared to go to any lengths for love. Jesus longs, just like any other human being, to know that he is important enough to another to have such gestures made on his behalf. But he also recognizes, immediately, that to test God's love in this way is to misunderstand God, and so to misunderstand himself, too. God is going to prove just how much Jesus means, not by the exclusivity of their relationship, but by the energy it makes available for others. Christians believe that Jesus used the knowledge that he is special to God to make everyone else know that they are, too.

Love is one of the central descriptions of what God is doing in the life and death of Jesus, but the love being described is not what most of our myths of love enable us to understand. 'For God so loved the world that he gave his only Son, so that everyone who believes in him may not perish but may have eternal life,' we are told (John 3:16). But what does it mean? Although it may seem odd to compare God and Jane Eyre, God's love is more like Jane's than we might imagine. Jane will not accept a love from Mr Rochester that will diminish either of them, and Rochester recognizes that he wants her to come to him freely, or not at all.

> 'And it is you, spirit – with your will and energy and virtue and purity – that I want; not alone your brittle frame. Of yourself, you could come with soft flight and nestle against my heart, if you would; seized against your will you will elude the grasp like an essence – you will vanish ere I inhale your fragrance.'

God sends Jesus into a world that is full of deceptions about love, some of them well-meaning and some of them simply vacuous or destructive. The world is full of people who long for love without any risk of it costing them anything. If love gets too demanding, we want to be able to back out. Or else we long for love that is exciting and makes us feel constantly excited, and when we begin to get bored, we start to look around for other things. And that is true not just of our longing for romantic love, but of all the different kinds of love in our lives. In our friendships, in our relationships with our families, in our emotions about our country or our football team, in whichever context we would use the word 'love', we are looking for a feeling of some kind, and get baffled and angry when, for long periods of time, there are no feelings, just a sense of being caught or bound to something or someone.

As Jesus comes to terms with what it is to be specially loved by God, he rejects the temptation to demand signs from God, and he lets go of his own need for feelings of excitement and joy. Instead, he begins his journey towards the cross. He takes upon himself the knowledge that being loved means you have something to give to others, and also that you have to teach others something of the reality of love. Like Jane Eyre, Jesus will not accept the simplistic, idolizing love that people are prepared to offer him when they think he is going to make their lives more exciting. Lots of people see Jesus as attractive and charismatic; they see him as someone who can change their lives and give them excitement and purpose, but on their own terms. Jesus refuses to be manipulated. Like Jane, he waits, offering his own tough brand of love, refusing to settle for anything less.

Most people are not impressed by Jesus' offer. If this is the love of God, they think, what is the point? They get angry and frustrated and, in the end, they just want to get rid of him. They shout out for his death, and are glad when his annoying offer of love is put to death on the cross.

Some people, though, get the point that love is not a

feeling, or not primarily so. It is a doing, a making, a path through life. You stay on it, whatever it brings, and you try to walk with others. When the Bible says that God loves the world so much that he sends us Jesus, it is giving us this new and challenging picture of love.

Love is patient; love is kind; love is not envious or boastful or arrogant or rude. It does not insist on its own way; it is not irritable or resentful; it does not rejoice in wrongdoing, but rejoices in the truth. It bears all things, believes all things, hopes all things, endures all things.

Love never ends. But as for prophecies, they will come to an end; as for tongues, they will cease; as for knowledge, it will come to an end. For we know only in part, and we prophesy only in part; but when the complete comes, the partial will come to an end. When I was a child, I spoke like a child, I thought like a child, I reasoned like a child; when I became an adult, I put an end to childish ways. For now we see in a mirror, dimly, but then we will see face to face. Now I know only in part; then I will know fully, even as I have been fully known. And now faith, hope, and love abide, these three; and the greatest of these is love.

---

1 CORINTHIANS 13:4–13

God's love for us, which starts when we are first made, is not sentimental. It is not designed to keep us safe, or to make us feel good. God loves us enough to want us to be creative, challenged, stretched and fulfilled beyond our wildest dreams. God's love wants us to be the biggest people we are capable of being. God dares us to join Jesus on the loving path that draws other people, too, into the enterprise. God is creating a permanent, loving and stable family, with room in it for anyone who is prepared to share this extraordinary 'doing' of love. This kind of love makes the people who shoulder it know that they are utterly special to God, beloved and central, just like Jesus. And the biggest thrill of such a love is when we can make other people know that they are special, too.

CHAPTER 5

Good Friday

As a child, it used to worry me horribly that Good Friday was called 'good'. I could not see what was good about the death of Jesus on the cross. My parents explained, patiently, year after year, that Jesus' death is good for us because it brings us forgiveness and salvation. But I always thought it was an odd way for God to achieve his purposes, and I persisted, stubbornly, in saying that, even if it was good for us – a question on which I reserved judgment – it still wasn't good for Jesus.

I allowed myself to be distracted by some of the things that our family customarily did on Good Friday, such as eating hot cross buns or making Easter gardens. The latter were particularly absorbing. First, you had to find a lid of a tin that had a little rim round the edge, to stop soil and water from simply running off. Then you put some earth on the lid and constructed a hill at one end for the three little crosses that you then made out of twigs. If you were at all artistic, you then covered the soil and hillside with grass, and planted such flowers in it as your parents would allow you to pick from the garden. There was generally some rivalry over this enterprise, though once it was done we quite quickly lost interest in our gardens and left them lying around, with their greenery wilting. I'm afraid that on more than one occasion our cat assumed that the gardens were there for other purposes altogether!

But fun as it was to make wonderfully lopsided buns and construct more or less lovely Easter gardens, I was still left with my doubts. And although after years of studying theology I might now give my children the answers my parents gave me, I still think the cross is one of the hardest things to explain.

The Bible description of Good Friday suggests that misunderstanding and confusion was a big part of the experience for many other people, too. Although Jesus had continually tried to warn the disciples about what was likely to happen to him, they simply could not take it in. They, like me, couldn't see why it was necessary and why someone who was so clearly special to God should have to die on the cross.

And during supper Jesus, knowing that the Father had given all things into his hands, and that he had come from God and was going to God, got up from the table, took off his outer robe, and tied a towel around himself. Then he poured water into a basin and began to wash the disciples' feet and to wipe them with the towel that was tied around him. He came to Simon Peter, who said to him, 'Lord, are you going to wash my feet?' Jesus answered, 'You do

not know now what I am doing, but later you will understand.' Peter said to him, 'You will never wash my feet.' Jesus answered, 'Unless I wash you, you have no share with me.' Simon Peter said to him, 'Lord, not my feet only but also my hands and my head!' Jesus said to him, 'One who has bathed does not need to wash, except for the feet, but is entirely clean. And you are clean, though not all of you.' For he knew who was to betray him; for this reason he said, 'Not all of you are clean.'

After he had washed their feet, had put on his robe, and had returned to the table, he said to them, 'Do you know what I have done to you? You call me Teacher and Lord – and you are right, for that is what I am. So if I, your Lord and Teacher, have washed your feet, you also ought to wash one another's feet. For I have set you an example, that you also should do as I have done to you. Very truly, I tell you, servants are not greater than their master, nor are messengers greater than the one who sent them. If you know these things, you are blessed if you do them.'

JOHN 13:2–17

The events of Good Friday really start on Thursday evening,
where so much is packed in that it is hard to remember that it all
happens in one night. First, Jesus and his friends have supper
together, then they go out to the Garden of Gethsemane, to pray.
The disciples already think the day has been long enough, and
they fall asleep, only to be wakened by the noise of a crowd, led
by their old friend Judas. Judas has betrayed Jesus and has
brought the authorities to arrest him. Jesus is taken away to
undergo a religious trial before being handed over to the civil
authorities for execution, first thing in the morning. All of this
happens between Thursday evening and Friday morning.

At the meal that takes place at the beginning of this eventful
period, Jesus tries again to explain what he is doing. He starts the
meal by taking off his outer clothes and getting down on his
knees and washing his friends' feet. In the hot dusty towns of
first-century Palestine, foot-washing was a real necessity. No one
would dream of coming inside and sitting down for a meal
without first washing off some of the filth and dust of the outside
world. But since it was hardly a pleasant task, it was usually the
job of a servant to wash his master's feet. But here is Jesus,
washing horrible, smelly feet, just like a common slave would do.
His disciples protest, rather belatedly offering to do the job
themselves, but Jesus says, oddly, that it is precisely because he is
their leader that he is performing this unpleasant function for
them. Leaders should be servants, he says.

You can see the disciples exchanging puzzled glances, their

eyebrows raised in slight exasperation. But they are used to Jesus
after all the time they have spent with him, and they simply nod
and head eagerly towards the dinner table. But even there, the
conversation is strange. Jesus offers them bread and wine, saying
that they represent his body and blood. Is that good or bad, the
disciples think? Does that mean they should be eating and drinking,
or not? And why does Jesus say that they are going to have to do
this again, in memory of him? Where is he going?

   Finally, one of the disciples, Judas, has had enough, and he
gets up and storms out of the room. Jesus seems to be expecting
this, too, and he won't let any of the others go after Judas to try
to bring him round. We don't know quite what motivates Judas,

and whether his frustration has been building up for a long time, or whether it has just been the last few days that have driven him to the edge. It is tempting to speculate that Judas longs for Jesus to be a success, and just can't bear the way he keeps going on about service and death instead. Judas has seen that Jesus has all the potential to be a proper leader. People love him and listen to him, and just a few weeks ago, they came out in huge numbers to cheer him through the streets of Jerusalem.

> **Many people spread their cloaks on the road, and others spread leafy branches that they had cut in the fields. Then those who went ahead and those who followed were shouting, 'Hosanna! Blessed is the one who comes in the name of the Lord! Blessed is the coming kingdom of our ancestor David! Hosanna in the highest heaven!'**

MARK 11:8–10

All the disciples could have been forgiven for thinking that at last Jesus was going to get going and start a proper revolution. But no, he allows the crowd's momentum to drain away, and then here he is, on this Thursday evening, washing feet like a servant and going on about suffering. Judas walks out and goes to Jesus' enemies and arranges to betray him.

Judas is confused about what Jesus is doing. The other disciples probably are, too, but they hide it better and go on with their supper. When Jesus decides after supper to go for a walk in the nearby Garden of Gethsemane, some of the disciples accompany him. But although they think they will keep Jesus company, they are soon fast asleep. Perhaps they had rather a lot to drink with their supper. Perhaps they have misjudged Jesus' mood. He sounded so calm, passing round the bread and wine, talking about death. The disciples had no reason to believe that the end was close – Jesus often talked to them about death, and they didn't really believe him. So when they wake up to the sound of shouts and realize that Judas has led a band of soldiers to Jesus, and they are taking him away, under arrest, the disciples are unprepared. They want to fight, to rescue Jesus, but he won't let them. At a complete loss, the disciples scatter. They have no idea what to do next, so they run away.

The people who are officially responsible for condemning Jesus to death are muddled, too. There are two trials, which take place between the Thursday night and the time when Jesus hangs on the cross. The first trial is conducted by the religious leaders. They know that they hate Jesus, and that they disagree with everything he says about God, but they can't quite put their finger on his offence. So they rig up a trial, with hired witnesses, who don't even bother to get their stories straight. Everybody knows what the outcome has to be. Jesus has to be found guilty of blasphemy, and then the state authorities have to be persuaded that he is a threat to them, too, so that they will carry out the sentence of death, which the religious leaders are not authorized to do.

They know that what will get the state governor, Pilate, worried is anything that challenges his own power. So they take Jesus to court, for the second of his trials. They say he is claiming to be the one who should be ruling the Jews. 'Are you a king?' Pilate asks Jesus. This is partly to gauge whether or not Jesus is a threat, but it also betrays Pilate's own interests. Pilate likes power, and is determined to hang on to it, even if it means

condemning an innocent man to death to preserve his own rule. But he quickly discovers that Jesus does not share that interest. 'What do you think a king is?' Jesus asks, in effect.

Pilate doesn't know it, but Jesus has already answered that question when he washed his disciples' feet. A king is someone who puts his people first – not Pilate's way at all. So Pilate loses interest, and sends Jesus off to be crucified.

Throughout this twenty-four hours, from Thursday evening until Jesus' death on Friday, no one really seems to know quite what they are doing, or why – except Jesus. At every stage of the proceedings, it could have gone so differently. Judas might have listened to what Jesus was saying as Jesus washed his feet, and he might have realized that Jesus was doing something revolutionary beyond Judas's wildest dreams. The religious leaders might have thought back over everything that Jesus had said about God and realized that it didn't mean they had to give up their beliefs, but just be willing to be more generous in their application. Pilate might have decided to be a proper ruler, and exercise his authority with justice, rather than just trying to maintain his own position. At any moment, if people had really understood what was going on, they might not have condemned Jesus to death.

There is a lovely, playful novel by Salley Vickers, called *Mr Golightly's Holiday*. Mr Golightly, we gradually realize as we read the book, is actually God the Father in disguise. He has come to stay in a small village on earth and to take a holiday. And the reason why he needs one is that he is baffled, and that is such an unusual position for God to be in that it has tired and depressed him. But his stay on earth doesn't really help. He simply finds himself getting involved with some of the people he meets, and caring about their well-being in a very direct way.

Finally one day, Mr Golightly and the devil meet on a hillside, and Mr Golightly begins to find out some truths that his God-likeness has so far shielded him from.

Mr Golightly said nothing but stood sunk in thought. It was true – hedged about, safe from turmoil, he had not been tested by life, and he had come to see that he had been the poorer thereby.

'I wonder,' he said, 'forgive me, there is no one else with whom I can have this discussion and it crosses my mind that perhaps you may be able to help me... I have been wondering very much about suffering and love. You see –'

'I understand,' the companion at his side interrupted, 'as the fountainhead yourself, you had no individual experience of it and yet –'

'And yet there is my son,' Mr Golightly broke in, not wanting the other to broach the name.

For the first time, his old rival turned to face him fully and his eyes looked like ruined stars. 'I was going to say,' he suggested mildly, 'that, from my rare observations of the phenomenon, to love another means in some sense to put oneself in their person; and for that to be possible there must first be the extinction of the self. I offer the idea in pure humility' – Mr Golightly gave a slight nod – 'this, perhaps is what your son –'

This is the thing that all the people around Jesus on Good Friday find so confusing. Like Mr Golightly, they cannot see what has been achieved by Jesus in submitting to his death. They do not understand that it is the culmination of what he has been doing all his life. By the end of his 'holiday', because Mr Golightly has learned to care and be changed by the people he has met, he has a much better understanding of his son. The Christian story is that Jesus chose to leave heaven and share our lives on earth, and at every stage of that sharing, he gave up some part of what could be seen as the real nature of divinity. He gave up rule and authority and security and dispassion, and chose to extinguish himself so as to identify completely with us.

Most of us will, out of love, give away something of ourselves and take risks for the people we love. But because what Jesus gives up on the cross is the life of God, that whole huge creative, dynamic power that brings the world into being, as he gives it up, he releases it. It is no longer bound up in him. It is available to be shared. And that is what Easter celebrates.

CHAPTER 6

Anger or Indifference

I always rather admire people who can express their anger, have a good shout and get it all out of their system. I can't do that. I generally try to pretend to myself that I'm really not angry at all. It is as though, with some part of myself, I don't believe that I'm allowed to be angry.

But sometimes anger is actually the appropriate reaction to something. It can be the opposite of a passive acceptance of an unjust situation. The energy that anger generates can propel us into action and make us work for change.

Charles Dickens was not afraid to express his anger at the inequalities he saw enshrined in Victorian society. He used his fiction to make his contemporaries see the poor and the outcast as real people. In *Bleak House*, for example, we read about a boy called Jo. He has no parents and no family of any kind, and he makes a bare living by sweeping crossings, which meant sweeping up the dirt and animal droppings that covered the roads. If he sweeps the road for a horse or a carriage to pass, the rider might occasionally throw him a tiny amount of money. But he is not seen as in any way a public servant, despite the usefulness of his task. He is constantly being 'moved on' by the police, who see only his poverty, and are afraid that it might be annoying to the well-off – as poverty still is. Many street people today know what it is to be 'moved on', so that the sight of them does not offend us.

Jo is someone so much on the margins of society that he can be ignored. He does not have to be thought of as a human being, and his society thinks it does not have to be judged by its treatment of him. Every society, to this day, has 'non-persons', who fall through all the nets of human community and can be treated as though they do not matter. A civilized society cannot

be found guilty of misusing people who don't really exist.

But Dickens makes Jo and his kind exist for us. We see Jo as an ordinary child, neglected and unloved, and it breaks our hearts. As Jo lies dying, Dr Woodcourt, one of the book's heroes, who is talking to Jo, says,

'It's turned wery dark, sir. Is there any light a-comin?'

'It is coming fast, Jo.'

Fast. The cart is shaken all to pieces, and the rugged road is very near its end.

'Jo, my poor fellow!'

'I hear you, sir, in the dark, but I'm a gropin – a gropin – let me catch hold of your hand.'

'Jo, can you say what I say?'

'I'll say anythink as you say, sir, for I knows it's good.'

'OUR FATHER.'

'Our Father! – yes, that's wery good, sir.'

'WHICH ART IN HEAVEN.'

'Art in heaven – is the light a-comin, sir?'

'It is close at hand. HALLOWED BE THY NAME!'

'Hallowed be – thy –'

The light is come upon the dark benighted way. Dead!

Dead, your Majesty. Dead, my lords and gentlemen. Dead, Right Reverends and Wrong Reverends of every order. Dead, men and women, born with heavenly compassion in your hearts. And dying thus around us every day.

Dickens's anger throbs through his closing words. He means us
to hear what we have all done to Jo and people like him as a
result of our indifference. He will not allow us to treat Jo as
though he is not human, not worth bothering about. As Dr
Woodcourt begins to teach Jo the Lord's Prayer, he is making
him part of the human family. In those days, every child of a
decent home in Britain would have been taught this prayer, and it
is one of the signs of Jo's outcast status that he does not know it.
But in his death, Dr Woodcourt wants him to know that he has
both a heavenly father and a human family, too. If we all have the
same heavenly father, we must belong together, Dr Woodcourt is
telling Jo. Now you belong, too, he is saying.

Not all anger is righteous anger, of course. Jesus is put to
death because he has made a lot of people angry by challenging
their vested interests. The religious leaders of his day don't like
the way he contradicts them and sets up his own authority over
theirs. The state officials don't like his apparent lack of respect
for their power, almost as though he doesn't think they are at all
important, and can't be bothered to compete with them for
something he doesn't value.

But Jesus' own anger, although rare, is more like Dickens's. It
is not the anger of hurt pride, like the religious and military leaders
display. It is the anger at injustice done, and at indifference
towards God.

The most famous incident the Bible tells us of Jesus losing his
temper is when he comes to the temple in Jerusalem and sees

that it has been turned into a kind of department store with a vaguely religious theme.

> Then Jesus entered the temple and drove out all who were selling and buying in the temple, and he overturned the tables of the money-changers and the seats of those who sold doves. He said to them, 'It is written, "My house shall be called a house of prayer"; but you are making it a den of robbers.'
> The blind and the lame came to him in the temple, and he cured them. But when the chief priests and the scribes saw the amazing things that he did, and heard the children crying out in the temple, 'Hosanna to the Son of David', they became angry and said to him, 'Do you hear what these are saying?' Jesus said to them, 'Yes, have you never read, "Out of the mouths of infants and nursing babies you have prepared praise for yourself"?'

MATTHEW 21:12–16

But if this is the most dramatic example, it is not the first time that Jesus has been angry with the people he believed were perverting God for their own ends. Several times in his ministry, when he goes to heal someone, he gets told off for it, either

because he is doing it on the sabbath, when they should all be
resting, or because he is taking away an infirmity that the
religious leaders had said was a punishment for sin. So Jesus
is issuing a direct challenge about what it is that religion is

supposed to be for. Then, as now, many religious people think that God should be invoked as a mechanism for controlling people, whereas Jesus sees God as a means of liberation.

So two kinds of anger come into conflict at the cross: Jesus' righteous anger at what has been done to people in the name of God; and the anger of the scribes and the pharisees, who are sure that they speak for God, and cannot bear to have their certainty and authority challenged in this way.

It looks as though the pharisees and priests are winning. Since they believe that power and control are part of what they are called to by God, they are not afraid to use it against Jesus. Jesus, meanwhile, is disabled by his unwillingness to use force. He will not let his disciples and supporters fight to free him, and there aren't enough of them to stand against the authorities and win by sheer weight of numbers, without the use of weapons. In the end, not enough people care enough to exercise their righteous anger on Jesus' behalf, whatever he may have done for them before.

Most of the crowds who mill around the scene of the crucifixion are indifferent to the issues involved. They know that they are seeing a travesty of justice, because they know that Jesus is not a criminal. But they know that life is full of injustice. If things are not always fair for them, why should they be for anyone else? Occasionally the crowds get quite excited, when they get an opportunity to shout and scream and let off some of their own pent-up frustration and anger at life. But their emotion

is entirely selfish. They can't be bothered to put themselves, imaginatively, in Jesus' place, just as most of Dickens's contemporaries did not want to have to see Jo as a real person.

Indifference allows so much. The best way to maintain indifference is to stay uninvolved and not find out too much about the people who might benefit if we started caring a little. So much of the inequality in our world is built on the indifference of those of us who are rich. We simply assume that our own needs are paramount. But we have very little idea of what the word 'need' might mean. If we allowed ourselves to find out about subsistence farming in Africa, for example, we might begin to understand 'need'. But that would make us uncomfortable; it might even make us angry enough to have to start working for change. And just look where that got Jesus!

Surely this is just how it is? We cannot all be filled with concern the whole time, can we? How would the world ever carry on? And anyway, what did Jesus really achieve with this righteous anger, and with this terrible compassion for every suffering person he met? He simply got himself crucified. What good could that do? This whole line of thought is simply going to make us feel guilty and uncomfortable, and that will make us angry in a completely unhelpful way, with a kind of angry frustration like that of the scribes and the pharisees of Jesus' day.

But Jesus claimed that his anger was God's, that God looks on the world with that kind of love, and that our indifference is the worst enemy of the divine. Those who struggle to free the

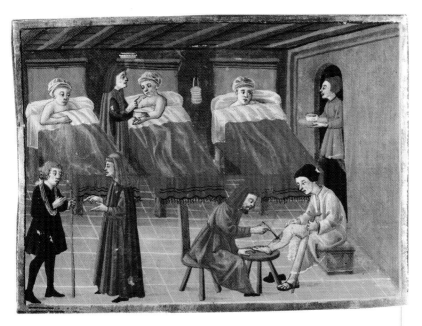

oppressed, feed the poor and heal the sick; those who sit beside a dying and frightened child and assure her that she is part of the loving human family of God; they are all singing with the rhythm with which the world was created. Whenever we draw another human being into our community, or refuse to allow groups of people to be treated as though they were hardly human and do not matter, we are demonstrating what we believe the world is for.

And if it sometimes seems that we are fighting a losing battle, and that inertia and brutality will always win, it is worth remembering that after Good Friday comes Easter. God always has a few more tricks up his sleeve than you realize.

CHAPTER 7

Fear and Complicity

Did you ever have a student teacher when you were a schoolchild? The one I remember particularly was quite young, and he had come to our school as part of his training to be a teacher. We were merciless with him. We mocked his acne and his accent, we openly discussed his sexual preferences, we constantly asked stupid and impertinent questions, and we made his life a misery. In the end, in one lesson, we actually reduced him to tears. I have no idea if he did go on to be a teacher, but I rather doubt it.

What I chiefly remember is how ashamed I felt, and I know that there were several others in the class who felt the same. We were longing for an excuse to stop the bullying, but we were too frightened. Teenage girls can be very cruel, and we would rather watch the innocent teacher being bullied than have that bullying turned back on us.

Pilate's state on Good Friday was not dissimilar. Pontius Pilate had the unenviable job of being the representative of the occupying power in Jerusalem. The Jews were a subject people, paying tax to the Roman Empire, and Pilate's job was to govern the land, to prevent any uprisings from succeeding, and to make sure that the money kept flowing into the Roman coffers.

When Jesus is brought to Pilate, Pilate knows that the religious leaders of Palestine have ganged up on Jesus for reasons that he doesn't quite understand, because he isn't really interested in the religious squabbles of this annoying group of people he has to rule. Pilate has to decide whether to co-operate with the scribes and pharisees and condemn Jesus to death, or whether to do his job as an impartial administrator of justice and let him go. That is not as straightforward a choice as it may sound. In the interests of long-term peace keeping, the goodwill of the local religious leaders was certainly more important than executing one troublesome man, even if he wasn't a threat to the state. But, in his heart of hearts, Pilate knows what he should do. If he starts giving in to these characters, he is in danger of losing their respect, as he is certainly in danger of losing his own.

Now at the festival the governor was accustomed to release a prisoner for the crowd, anyone whom they wanted. At that time they had a notorious prisoner, called Jesus Barabbas. So after they had gathered, Pilate said to them, 'Whom do you want me to release for you, Jesus Barabbas or Jesus who is

called the Messiah?' For he realized that it was out of jealousy that they had handed him over. While he was sitting on the judgement seat, his wife sent word to him, 'Have nothing to do with that innocent man, for today I have suffered a great deal because of a dream about him.' Now the chief priests and the elders persuaded the crowds to ask for Barabbas and to have Jesus killed. The governor again said to them, 'Which of the two do you want me to release for you?' And they said, 'Barabbas.' Pilate said to them, 'Then what should I do with Jesus who is called the Messiah?' All of them said, 'Let him be crucified!' Then he asked, 'Why, what evil has he done?' But they shouted all the more, 'Let him be crucified!'

So when Pilate saw that he could do nothing, but rather that a riot was beginning, he took some water and washed his hands before the crowd, saying, 'I am innocent of this man's blood; see to it yourselves.'

MATTHEW 27:15–24

But Pilate does give in, through fear of a riot, through laziness, through the simple reality that he doesn't care very much about Jesus. Whatever his wife may say, Pilate never expects to hear any

more of the matter. He can hardly know that this is to become
his chief claim to fame for 2,000 years afterwards: that he could
have saved Jesus and he chose not to.

Most of us have at one time or another done something that
we really knew we shouldn't have done, or have co-operated,
through laziness and fear, in allowing something to happen when
we could have prevented it. We may persuade ourselves that we
are not doing wrong on the same scale as Pilate, but the salutary
truth is that Pilate didn't think what he was doing was *terribly*
wrong. He knew it wasn't quite right, but it was part of his job to

make hard, realistic decisions, and Jesus was by no means the first person he had had to send for execution and he wouldn't be the last. When we are in the middle of things, we are not always the best judges of what the consequences will be. We can deceive ourselves into thinking that we are acting for the best, and hide our own motives, even from ourselves, so that we do not have to admit that we just cannot be bothered to do what is right.

In C. S. Lewis's fantasy adventure story, *The Lion, the Witch and the Wardrobe*, Edmund, one of the four children who find their way accidentally into a magical land, has quarrelled with his brother and sisters, and he is about to betray them to the evil queen, the White Witch. He is determined not to let himself see that what he is doing is completely unjustified. Instead, he persuades himself that the others deserve it for the way they have treated him.

As for what the Witch would do with the others, he didn't want her to be particularly nice to them... but he managed to believe, or to pretend he believed, that she wouldn't do anything very bad to them, 'Because,' he said to himself, 'all these people who say nasty things about her are her enemies and probably half of it isn't true. She was jolly nice to me, anyway, much nicer than they are. I expect she is the rightful Queen really...' At least, that was the excuse he made in his own mind for what he was doing. It wasn't a very good excuse, however, for deep down inside him he really knew that the White Witch was bad and cruel.

Actions have consequences and they are not all foreseeable. Edmund does not know, as he stands grumpily and bitterly in the snow, that the great Lion, who is the saviour-figure of Narnia, will have to be sacrificed to save the land from the consequences of Edmund's betrayal.

Not all consequences are so terrible. Peter, one of Jesus' disciples, also does something on Good Friday that is to make history, but he is fortunate to come out of it as the hero in the end.

Then they seized him and led him away, bringing him into the high priest's house. But Peter was following at a distance. When they had kindled a fire in the middle of the courtyard and sat down together, Peter sat among them. Then a servant-girl, seeing him in the firelight, stared at him and said, 'This man also was with him.' But he denied it, saying, 'Woman, I do not know him.' A little later someone else, on seeing him, said, 'You also are one of them.' But Peter said, 'Man, I am not!' Then about an hour later yet another kept insisting, 'Surely this man also was with him; for he is a Galilean.' But Peter said, 'Man, I do not know what you are talking about!' At that moment, while he was still speaking, the cock crowed. The Lord turned and looked at Peter. Then Peter remembered the word of the Lord, how he had said to him,

'Before the cock crows today, you will deny me three times.' And he went out and wept bitterly.

LUKE 22:54–62

Peter has been with Jesus as long as any of the disciples, and he thinks of himself as one of Jesus' best and most devoted followers, brave and trustworthy. When Jesus is arrested in the Garden of Gethsemane on Thursday night, Peter decides to follow and see where Jesus is being taken.

You can picture him, sneaking along behind the thugs who are dragging Jesus away. Peter ducks and darts, he jumps behind bushes and peeps out, he runs from one place of cover to the next, imagining that he is being inconspicuous. In his mind's eye, he is rather like a character in a play, and he is still all fired up with the adrenalin of the fight in the Garden of Gethsemane. He's not quite sure what he plans to do when he gets into the courtyard where they are taking Jesus, but he's confident he will think of something, because, after all, he's Peter; he always comes up with a plan. Perhaps he will charge in, grab Jesus and rescue him before his enemies know what is going on. Or perhaps he will just be there to back Jesus up, when Jesus takes action. After all, Jesus seemed to be expecting something like this, so he's probably got it covered. Good old Peter, Jesus will say, always there when I need him. How red-faced all the others will be, when Peter and Jesus swagger home, victorious. Cunningly, incredibly bravely, Peter goes right into the enemy stronghold and begins to mingle, daringly, secretly, with the enemy forces.

But then it all begins to go horribly wrong. For one thing, all the so-called enemy troops are not troops at all; they're just servants, sitting round a fire, slightly bored, but prepared to kill the time with a bit of conversation before bed. It would be silly to pick a fight with a girl cooking the dinner. Deprived of action, Peter's courage begins to drain out of him, and he is horribly afraid.

He tells himself, of course, that he's afraid for his own safety.

It's very hard to tell if his fear is justified. The men who came to arrest Jesus took no notice at all of the disciples who were with him at the time. They presumably could have rounded them all up, if they had wanted to, but there is no suggestion that they did. And these servants sitting round the fire are clearly pretty sure that Peter *is* a follower of Jesus, whatever he says, but they take no action. They are content just to tease him. No, I think that Peter has generated his own fear, and it isn't really fear for his own physical safety. He's afraid that this is the end, that there really is not going to be a sudden rescue, that he has really lost Jesus for ever. As long as he can see Jesus, he is brave; but left to himself, he is lost.

Although he doesn't know it, Peter's fear and failure are precisely the things that are going to qualify him to lead the Church. He has discovered that the one thing he cannot live without is Jesus. He has discovered that, by himself, he is neither brave nor faithful nor resourceful. In the years to come, everyone will hear this story of how Peter betrayed Jesus out of fear, and they will see Peter afraid again, and wrong again, and Peter really won't care. He will know that his history makes him the perfect witness, and that through his testimony, many people will come to Jesus. Because of Peter, they will come to faith, knowing that faith is not a guarantee that we will always be right, or that we will never be afraid. Faith is not something earned by the deserving. It is the gift of Jesus, whom we will never have to lose, even if we betray him.

It is hard not to look at the cross with fear. Like Peter, it is hard not to see it as the end of all our self-obsessed play-acting. Most of the time, we can swagger about, playing at being good people who would never stand by and let someone else suffer without coming to their aid. We don't expect to have to make huge sacrifices for others, because it is the job of the government or the legal system or even God to make sure that ultimately justice prevails. We cannot be expected to do that on our own.

But when it comes to something like the cross, where we are required to stand up and be counted, our fear sets in. Perhaps Pilate and Peter are actually very similar to us, and in the depths of our fear we too might be prepared to turn a blind eye to injustice and betray Jesus, and others, in order to guarantee our own safety.

In the sixteenth century in England, when King Henry VIII had decided to separate the Church in England from the Catholic Church, a group of people from the north of England decided to march to London and beg the King to reconsider. This valiant company, the Pilgrimage of Grace, was led by a man called Robert Aske, and their story is told by H. F. M. Prescott in a book called *Man on a Donkey*. At first it appeared that it was going to be successful. Aske met the King and was given his assurance that all would be well, so he disbanded his troops and waited for the King to keep his promise. But the King had no intention of doing so, and soon Aske was hanging in chains, abandoned by his King and, he believed, by his God.

And as his eye told him of the sickening depth below his body, and as his mind foreknew the lagging endlessness of torment before him, so, as if the lightning had brought an inner illumination also, he knew the greater gulf of despair above which his spirit hung, helpless and aghast.

God did not now, nor would in any furthest future, prevail. Once He had come, and died. If He came again, again He would die, and again, and so for ever, by His own will rendered powerless against the free and evil wills of men.

Then Aske met the full assault of darkness without reprieve of hoped for light, for God ultimately vanquished was no God at all. But yet, though God was not God, as the head of the dumb worm turns, so his spirit turned, blindly, gropingly, hopelessly loyal, towards that good, that holy, that merciful, which though not God, though vanquished, was still the last dear love of a vanquished and tortured man.

Looking at the cross, we need to make Peter's and Robert Aske's discovery. There are some things worse than fear for our own safety. Fear of being without love, for example, without meaning in life, without self-respect. We are very much afraid of what might be asked of us in defence of these things, but that fear pales into insignificance beside the fear of being without them. That's what Peter discovers when he has denied Jesus for the third time, and it makes him weep bitterly. He would rather be afraid with Jesus, who represents to Peter all that makes life meaningful, than safe, with nothing.

CHAPTER 8

Compassion and Love

As a very small child at boarding school, I discovered that there is more than one way to show kindness to someone. I was very homesick and unhappy to begin with, and I thought that the people who would help most were the ones who were suffering the same emotions as I was. And, indeed, it was wonderfully comforting to sit and hold hands and cry with someone who was equally homesick. But the trouble was that although we could sympathize with each other and share our pain, we couldn't, in the end, offer each other any hope that we would ever feel better. So the other, more surprising, kind of person who could help was the kind of schoolfriend who seemed happy and sorted out, who seemed to have found a way not just to survive at boarding school, but even to flourish.

Although it may seem impossible to imagine, while Jesus is hanging on the cross on Good Friday, there is hanging beside him a man who seems able to be kind and cheerful even in conditions

of extreme agony. He could not, of course, offer any hope of survival, since he, too, was going to die. But he could keep alive to the end the steadfast belief that death cannot make you behave against your nature. You can still be compassionate and human even while hanging on a cross.

Two others also, who were criminals, were led away to be put to death with him. When they came to the place that is called The Skull, they crucified Jesus there with the criminals, one on his right and one on his left. Then Jesus said, 'Father, forgive them;

for they do not know what they are doing.' And they cast lots to divide his clothing. And the people stood by, watching; but the leaders scoffed at him, saying, 'He saved others; let him save himself if he is the Messiah of God, his chosen one!' The soldiers also mocked him, coming up and offering him sour wine, and saying, 'If you are the King of the Jews, save yourself!' There was also an inscription over him, 'This is the King of the Jews.'

One of the criminals who were hanged there kept deriding him and saying, 'Are you not the Messiah? Save yourself and us!' But the other rebuked him, saying, 'Do you not fear God, since you are under the same sentence of condemnation? And we indeed have been condemned justly, for we are getting what we deserve for our deeds, but this man has done nothing wrong.' Then he said, 'Jesus, remember me when you come into your kingdom.' He replied, 'Truly I tell you, today you will be with me in Paradise.'

LUKE 23:32–43

All three men are condemned to die by a society that has decided to give up on them and treat them as valueless. They can no longer contribute usefully to society and can therefore be disposed of. The first criminal has accepted the rest of society's judgment upon Jesus, and, by implication, upon himself, too. He has nothing at all to gain by joining in the tormenting of Jesus, but he does it anyway. He believes that he and Jesus are outside the human community, officially non-existent, and about to be actually non-existent, so it really doesn't matter how they treat each other.

But the other criminal has refused to allow his life or his horrible death to dehumanize him. He has refused to become what his judges told him he was – a non-person. He accepts punishment for the crime he has committed against his brothers and sisters, but his acceptance is part of his affirmation that he still belongs in the company of human society. The people he has wronged are real to him, and he believes he is still real to them, even as he hangs in unbearable pain on the cross.

When he turns to Jesus and says, 'Jesus, remember me when you come into your kingdom,' we have no reason to believe that he has suddenly been converted. It seems much more likely that he is simply being kind to the man beside him, sharing his fate. He does know that Jesus hasn't done anything wrong and has simply had the misfortune to get caught up in the machinery. But he knows that happens. Jesus isn't the first and he won't be the last innocent man to be put to death. But at least he can die with the sound of a few kind words ringing in his ears.

It is hard for us to imagine the kind of pain the three men on the crosses must have been experiencing, and so quite what an effort it took to remain sane and kind under those circumstances. We know from other horrific situations, such as the Nazi extermination camps, or the genocidal villages in Rwanda, that such compassion can be found amid the bestial violence that human beings do to one another.

But how extraordinary that here on the cross, God asks for our compassion. How will we respond? We may long for God to behave in a properly God-like way, and to be powerful and protective, but he tells us that that will not make us the people

we are called to be. As we respond in compassion to the suffering Jesus, and to other suffering human beings, we begin to discover what makes us most truly human: our ability to respond to the humanity of others. Every time we act with compassion towards someone else, we bring them into our society. We acknowledge them as human beings, like ourselves, with needs and feelings just like our own. Compassion refuses to allow us to treat each other as though we are of no account, as though we do not really exist. We recognize that we as individuals and as a human community are properly judged by how many others we can share our humanity with.

That's why Jesus is able to make this extraordinary promise to the criminal beside him: 'Truly I tell you, today you will be with me in Paradise.' The criminal has done the only thing necessary. He has seen another human being's need and responded to it. He has refused to dehumanize Jesus and so he has established his own real humanity, too.

This compassionate thief thought he was just giving Jesus enough courage and hope to face his death with dignity. He thought he was doing the giving, but instead he received. So many of us could tell a similar story, though perhaps not in such dramatic circumstances. We may start to act generously out of duty or shame, slightly grudgingly, hoping we will not have to do too much. And then we find, to our amazement, that being allowed to give is one of the best feelings in the world. Generosity and compassion make us feel more human, more alive, as though this is what we are meant to be here for.

Perhaps this is part of the answer to my childhood anxiety, which was feeling that although Good Friday might be 'good' for us, it certainly cannot be said to be 'good' for Jesus. Perhaps, after all, it might be good for both of us. We see the human, suffering, agonized figure of Jesus, for those hours of pain not looking like God, not looking like our creator who has no need of anything we might have to offer. He simply looks like any

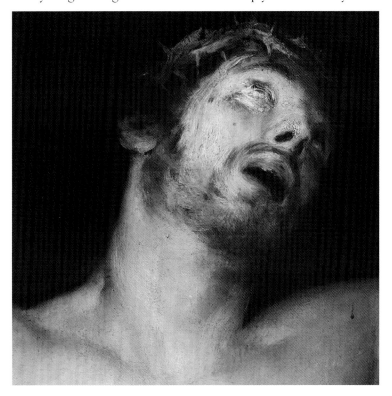

other suffering human being, and we long to help him. Like the thief dying beside him, we long to do or say something that could offer at least a crumb of comfort in this terrible situation.

The medieval English mystical writer, Julian of Norwich, in *Revelations of Divine Love*, suggests that we should allow God to be generous to us, too.

> *Then said our good Lord Jesus Christ: Art thou well pleased that I suffered for thee? I said: Yea, good Lord, I thank thee: Yea, good Lord, blessed mayst thou be. Then said Jesus, our kind Lord: If thou art pleased, I am pleased. It is a joy, a bliss, an endless satisfying to me that ever suffered I Passion for thee; and if I might suffer more, I would suffer more. Wherefore we be not only his by his buying, but also by the courteous gift of his Father, we be his bliss, we be his meed, we be his worship, we be his crown. (And this was a singular marvel and a full delectable beholding, that we be his crown!) This that I say is so great bliss to Jesus that he setteth at nought all his travail, and his hard Passion and his cruel and shameful death.*

Julian is not trying to say that it gives God a kind of twisted pleasure to suffer for us, but that if suffering is the only way to achieve what must be done, then he is happy to do it, so great is his love for us. The cross is all of a piece with what the Bible suggests about the character of God all along. When God makes the world, inbuilt in it for us is the choice of whether or not to believe, whether or not to obey God. In all the dealings between

God and people, that remains the pattern. God could force people, but then they would be like slaves or automata. They would not be the living, creative beings God made to share in the divine life and joy. God allows us to make bitter and painful mistakes, and the cross shows us very starkly what we are capable of.

We are capable of hating and rejecting Jesus, who has done nothing wrong, only spoken about the loving presence of God. We are so afraid of that challenge that we would rather kill Jesus than face God and the reality of ourselves.

Jesus accepts what we do to him. He says to his disciples, when they want to fight to rescue him, 'Do you think that I cannot appeal to my Father, and he will at once send me more than twelve legions of angels?' (Matthew 26:53). Jesus does not choose to save himself. He chooses to accept our judgment on what he has offered us in his life, all he has said and done and promised in the name of God.

But just when we think we have won, we find that we have lost the thing that mattered to us most. We find that we have lost our humanity. We look at the dying figure on the cross, or the starving children of Africa, or the shanty towns of Latin America, and we know that we have helped to do this and we are the poorer for it.

Simply in human terms, it makes sense to relieve suffering. If we can reduce the world's poverty, we will make it a safer place for all of us. There will be fewer threats of war; we will begin to be able to work together on the environmental issues that will otherwise ruin life for all our children and grandchildren. We may be very slightly poorer in material terms, but think of how much we will gain!

If this is what happens when we allow compassion and love to guide our actions towards each other, and work together, what might not happen if we start to work with God? On the cross on Good Friday, Jesus accepts and absorbs all our anger and hatred and fear, and gives us back only compassion and forgiveness and love. His cross becomes a kind of black hole into which all our

empty nothingness can be pulled.

What is released from that action of Jesus at Easter is the massive burst of life and energy that we call the resurrection. We cannot make it happen, because it is more than we are capable of. But we can co-operate with it. We can begin to believe in the possibility of transformation, because we did the worst we were capable of on Good Friday, but Jesus suffered it for love of us and gave us back our true selves, made in the image of God, made to create and re-create out of love, just as God does.

Man on a Donkey is a story set in the reign of King Henry VIII of England. One of the saddest characters in it is a priest called Gib Dawe, who longs to be a fiery, successful preacher, but who simply does not like either himself or other people enough to be any good. He will not co-operate with God's life pouring out from the cross, because he simply cannot believe it is that easy. He believes that because he is like a bucket so full of holes that it cannot be any use, he can do nothing.

He did not know that though the bucket be leaky it matters not at all when it is deep in the deep sea, and the water both without it and within. He did not know, because he was too proud to know, that a man must endure to sink, and sink again, but always crying upon God, never for shame ceasing to cry, until the day when he shall find himself lifted by the bland swell of that power, inward, secret, as little to be known as to be doubted, the power of omnipotent grace in tranquil irresistible operation.

CHAPTER 9

Waiting

When I was a small child, we lived in India. One of my most abiding memories of India is of people waiting. There was an immense patience and immobility about the large crowds of people waiting in the hot sun for a train that would come when it was good and ready. Timetables were always rather notional, partly due to the huge distances covered. Whole families would come with their cooking pots and bedding, and simply camp out on and around the station until their train came. They couldn't go home, because they didn't know when the train would arrive, and anyway, they had often already travelled some distance to reach the station, and couldn't afford to go away and come back again. Poor people have very little choice about waiting, because they cannot afford to buy themselves other options. They just have to wait and hope.

Although the station could seem calcified in inertia, however, at the very first sound of the approaching train it would come to life. The vendors would pick up their wares and jostle for position so as to get closest to the first-class compartments. The waiting families would begin to assemble their property and their

children and prepare to do battle for their seats. Station officials would emerge, hastily buttoning their uniforms, ready to greet the train and see it on its way.

Each train always seemed already full to bursting as it arrived at the station, but somehow all the waiting hordes would be accommodated, and the train would set off. The station would sink back into patient anticipation, as would the travellers on the train, for the journey would probably take days.

The last few days of Jesus' life involve just that pattern of inaction followed by mad activity. The activity generally comes from people who are not directly involved in the story – for example, the crowds who mill around the foot of the cross, enjoying the spectacle of someone else's suffering, and displaying what they imagine to be their great wit as they shout and jeer at the men hanging on the cross. But there are long periods where the crowds are just waiting: waiting for the outcome of the various trials, waiting for the soldiers to bring out the prisoners. The crowds can't really influence events much; they just have to wait.

The soldiers are busy. They have to hustle the prisoners along and they have to guard them, in case anyone tries to rescue them, or in case they try to make a break for it. They

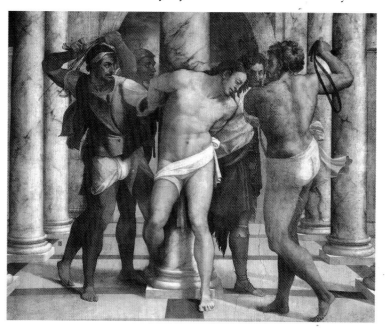

have to organize the mechanics of the crucifixion, checking that the crosses and nails are strong enough to do the job, and then they have to oversee the grisly business of hauling down the bodies and disposing of them. There is quite a lot of just standing about in between times, while the commanders make the decisions, or while the men hanging on the cross take their time dying. The soldiers are under orders: they are busy when they are told to be, and they wait when they are told to wait.

But Jesus and the disciples can do very little in these last hours. Jesus is pushed around from one place to another while other people decide his fate, and the disciples hang around the edges of the scene, in an agony of impatience and impotence. There is nothing they can do except wait and see what happens.

And then there is the terrible time while Jesus is hanging on the cross, waiting for death. There is nothing he can do to hasten his body's processes; he simply has to wait until his body decides it cannot cope with suffering any more, and gives up. Some of the people who love him, his mother and some of the disciples, are also waiting with longing impatience for death to release him from his torture.

After Jesus is dead, his followers do not realize that they are waiting. After all, what else is there to wait for? Everything is over. Perhaps they feel that they are waiting for their own pain to diminish, their own sense of loss and bereavement to become bearable. Only time can do that, but the leaden hours go so slowly to the recently bereaved. Jesus' followers are sharing that experience with all of us who have lost loved ones.

What exactly is Jesus doing in that strange twilight time between Friday afternoon and resurrection day on Sunday? What is happening in the cool darkness of the tomb? What is the point of this strange lull? Why does God not raise Jesus from the dead at once, in immediate repudiation of the power of death to hold on to the beloved Son of God?

This waiting between Good Friday and Easter Day confirms the reality of Jesus' death. He does not temporarily faint, and revive a few hours later. He genuinely lies in the grave, dead. The disciples have to face that reality: Jesus is dead. Whatever they thought he was doing, with their help, is over. In the days after the crucifixion, they go over and over in their heads all that they

have seen and heard of Jesus, trying to make sense of it. By the time they meet the risen Jesus, they no longer expect the wild revolutionary excitement of the years of Jesus' earthly ministry. They know that they have got it wrong before, and they wait this time to hear what Jesus has to tell them. They wait to get their instructions. The disciples who meet the risen Jesus seem a much quieter, more sober group of people. Waiting has taught them patience.

They had thought that they were vital to Jesus' enterprise, but now they suspect that, since they don't actually have a clue what is going on, they can't be as important as they originally thought. Conversations between Jesus and the disciples before the crucifixion are generally characterized by a great deal of baffled questioning, but after the resurrection, the disciples are much more silent and awed. God has done something extraordinary, without any help from them at all. Perhaps they are no longer necessary.

When the poet John Milton went blind, he wrote movingly about his sense of waste. He believed that God had given him one talent – to write poetry – and that his blindness was preventing him from exercising it.

> When I consider how my light is spent,
> Ere half my days, in this dark world and wide,
> And that one talent which is death to hide
> Lodged with me useless, though my soul more bent

To serve therewith my Maker, and present
My true account, lest he returning chide,
'Doth God exact day-labour, light denied?'
I fondly ask. But Patience, to prevent
That murmur, soon replies: 'God doth not need
Either man's work or his own gifts; who best
Bear his mild yoke, they serve him best. His state
Is kingly; thousands at his bidding speed,
And post o'er land and ocean without rest;
They also serve who only stand and wait.'

Milton has no idea how it can serve God to have him standing around, waiting, but then he doesn't know how all the others who are rushing round the world are serving God, either. He has to learn to wait simply because there is no alternative, and where there is no alternative, that is the service asked of us.

Waiting is one of the most difficult tasks we have to face, because it makes us feel so helpless. In most areas of our lives, we are used to being able to make decisions and choices that will make things happen for us. Our day-to-day lives are so full of things to be done, that we imagine it would be lovely to have a period of waiting, where things are taken out of our hands and there is nothing we can do.

But when we are actually presented with a situation where the only thing we can do is wait, we find it intensely difficult. When we or someone we love is ill, there is a lot of waiting – in hospital rooms, waiting for test results, waiting to see if treatment works. This kind of waiting is almost unbearable, because all our choice is taken away. We cannot make things happen by our energy or force of will. This painful waiting is a hard lesson in reality. Facing what cannot be changed is part of the world. Sometimes we cannot wriggle or negotiate things round to the way we want them to be, and then to stand and wait is indeed the only service we can give. It is a service to reality and so to ourselves.

In the early days of the Christian Church, St Paul gets quite cross with people who think they know everything about the faith and are not prepared to wait and learn, and be fed by the experience of others. He says they are like babies, still only capable of digesting milk. They have to be patient.

And so, brothers and sisters, I could not speak to you as spiritual people, but rather as people of the flesh, as infants in Christ. I fed you with milk, not solid food, for you were not ready for solid food. Even now you are still not ready, for you are still of the flesh. For as long as there is jealousy and quarrelling among you, are you not of the flesh, and behaving according to human inclinations?

---

1 Corinthians 3:1–3

Just as the disciples mature as they wait, helplessly, to see what God is doing without them, so we can all mature by accepting what we cannot change. As we look at the reality we are given, who knows what future we are being prepared for? If we choose to retreat from what we cannot change, to retreat back into a fantasy life, where we deny the reality of anything we cannot control, the chances are that we are making ourselves less and less ready to take up the next exciting challenge we might be offered.

For most of his ministry, Jesus seems to be a man very much in control. He talks and acts with enormous assurance and authority. The crowds who follow him don't know that this strength is born out of that period of waiting in the desert, after his baptism; waiting to find out who he is and what God needs from him. Perhaps it is what he learned through that waiting that enables him to face the enforced waiting of the cross and the grave.

There is a tradition that during that period of waiting between the crucifixion and the resurrection, Jesus goes to the place of the dead, to end the waiting of the thousands whose lives are over, and who are sitting in the patience of death. They no longer have any choices, but because of all the choices Jesus has already made, and because he has been prepared not to choose, but to wait in suffering and death, we can imagine that he is able to bring others back into life and freedom. This is called 'the harrowing of hell', and is memorably described by Edmund Spenser in his 'Amoretti' poetry:

Most glorious Lord of life, that on this day
didst make thy triumph over death and sin;
and having harrowed hell, didst bring away
captivity thence captive us to win...
So let us love, dear love, like as we ought,
love is the lesson which the Lord us taught.

CHAPTER 10

Easter

From my childhood, I don't remember the kind of Easter associations that my children now have, which are often due more to clever marketing practices than to the Christian Easter message. There is one particular custom that my children enjoy, which I do envy, and that is Easter egg hunts. I remember especially the Easter egg hunt which used to take place in the grounds of our cathedral in Wales, after the Easter morning services. The choirboys and all the younger members of the congregation would go hunting, with squeals of joy, among the old tombstones and long grass of the cathedral churchyard. It seemed to me a very good symbol, that they should be looking for eggs, which symbolize new life, among the headstones. Looking for life where you would expect death is one of the characteristics of Easter.

Easter starts very early in the morning in the Bible stories. A lot of churches celebrate this with services either late at night or very early in the morning, kindling the new fire, the new life of Easter, with the flames showing brightly against the darkness around.

All the stories of the resurrection agree that the first people to find out that Jesus was no longer dead were a group of women, in the early dawn light. They had been friends and followers of Jesus, and they had got up very early, before other people would be stirring, to go to his tomb and clean and sweeten his body, as their last act of love for him. We can picture them, stumbling along, tired and grief-stricken, but determined to do this thing for Jesus. But when they get to the tomb, the body is gone. Instead, they find a strange man sitting guarding the entrance to

the tomb, who tells them that Jesus has risen from the dead, and that they are to go and tell his other disciples what has happened. The women do as they are told, but, perhaps not unnaturally, the other disciples don't believe them. At last, Peter goes to check out their story, and finds the empty tomb, and the cloths that should have been wrapped around the dead body lying neatly in the tomb.

In itself, this could only lead to the conclusion that someone had stolen Jesus' body, for some unknown reason. But then there follows a series of meetings between Jesus and his followers. They are clearly meetings with the real Jesus, but his body, although physical, behaves strangely. It is not always present, and it is not always recognizable.

Mary Magdalene, for example, who was one of the women who went early in the morning to the tomb to care for the dead body of Jesus, simply cannot bear it when she fails to find it. We find her standing in the garden where the tomb is, crying. She just wants to know what has happened to Jesus. She would be satisfied if she could just see him, even if he is dead.

As she cries, she sees a man, whom she takes for the gardener, the person whose job it is to look after the graveyard. He seems a kind man, and asks her what the matter is. But she is now so overwrought that she suspects everybody, and she practically accuses him of stealing Jesus' body.

But Mary stood weeping outside the tomb. As she wept, she bent over to look into the tomb; and she saw two angels in white, sitting where the body of Jesus had been lying, one at the head and the other at the feet. They said to her, 'Woman, why are you weeping?' She said to them, 'They have taken away my Lord, and I do not know where they have laid him.' When she had said this, she turned round and saw Jesus standing there, but she did not know that it was Jesus. Jesus said to her, 'Woman, why are you weeping? For whom are you looking?' Supposing him to be the gardener, she said to him, 'Sir, if you have carried him away, tell me where you have laid him, and I will take him away.' Jesus said to her, 'Mary!' She turned and said to him in Hebrew, 'Rabbouni!' (which means Teacher). Jesus said to her, 'Do not hold on to me, because I have not yet ascended to the Father. But go to my brothers and say to them, "I am ascending to my Father and your Father, to my God and your God." '

JOHN 20:11–17

It seems extraordinary that Mary, who has been so close to Jesus and who is thinking of no one but Jesus, doesn't recognize him. There is clearly something a bit different about him now. But his voice hasn't changed. As soon as he says her name, Mary knows him and rushes towards him. But Jesus has not come back from the dead in order to continue his old life just as it was. Everything is going to be different now, and Mary is the first to learn that the new life of Jesus is not just for his disciples and friends, but for everyone. This is the life of God, who made all life from the very beginning and is now going to remake it again.

The seventeenth-century Anglican preacher, Lancelot Andrewes, says that Mary was actually more correct than she realized in thinking that Jesus was the gardener.

A gardener he is. The first, the fairest garden that ever was, paradise, he was the gardener, for it was of his planning. And ever since it is he as God makes all our gardens green, sends all the herbs and flowers we then gather... Christ rising was indeed a gardener, and that a strange one, who made such an herb grow out of the ground this day as the like was never seen before, a dead body to shoot forth alive out of the grave.

But I ask, was he so this day alone? No, but this profession of his, this day begun, he will follow to the end. For he it is that by virtue of

this morning's act shall garden our bodies, too, turn all our graves into garden plots; yea, shall one day turn land and sea and all into a great garden, and so husband them as they shall in due time bring forth live bodies, even all our bodies alive again.

Andrewes is pulling together all kinds of Easter themes in this one sermon on Mary Magdalene. He is talking of God the creator, of Jesus' death and resurrection, of spring and of our own deaths and hopes for life after death. And, just in passing, he mentions the strange 'herb' that Jesus' resurrection body is. It is so strange that Mary does not recognize it at once. Nor is she the only one.

Now on that same day two of them were going to a village called Emmaus, about seven miles from Jerusalem, and talking with each other about all these things that had happened. While they were talking and discussing, Jesus himself came near and went with them, but their eyes were kept from recognizing him. And he said to them, 'What are you discussing with each other while you walk along?' They stood still, looking sad. Then one of them, whose name was Cleopas, answered him, 'Are you the only stranger in Jerusalem who does not know the things that have taken place there in these days?' He asked them, 'What things?' They

replied, 'The things about Jesus of Nazareth, who was a prophet mighty in deed and word before God and all the people, and how our chief priests and leaders handed him over to be condemned to death and crucified him. But we had hoped that he was the one to redeem Israel. Yes, and besides all this, it is now the third day since these things took place. Moreover, some women of our group astounded us. They were at the tomb early this morning, and when they did not find his body there, they came back and told us that they had indeed seen a vision of angels who said that he was alive. Some of those who were with us went to the tomb and found it just as the women had said; but they did not see him.' Then he said to them, 'Oh, how foolish you are, and how slow of heart to believe all that the prophets have declared! Was it not necessary that the Messiah should suffer these things and then enter into his glory?' Then beginning with Moses and all the prophets, he interpreted to them the things about himself in all the scriptures.

As they came near to the village to which they were going, he walked ahead as if he were going on. But they urged him strongly, saying, 'Stay with us, because it is almost evening and the day is now

nearly over.' So he went in to stay with them. When he was at the table with them, he took bread, blessed and broke it, and gave it to them. Then their eyes were opened, and they recognized him...

LUKE 24:13–31

Just after Jesus' death, when rumours about his resurrection are beginning to circulate, two of his followers are walking along a road, talking about everything that has been happening. Another traveller catches up with them while they walk, and soon they are telling him all about it, too. To their amazement, he seems to

think that they should have expected it all, both the death and the resurrection of their leader. He starts quoting Scripture to them, all the texts that suddenly click into place. The two disciples can't bear to let him go. They just have to hear more, and they pretty well force the stranger to stay the night with them and continue the discussion over dinner. But as they sit down, the man takes bread and breaks it, ready to share, and suddenly they recognize Jesus.

For Mary, it is Jesus' voice; for these two disciples, it is the action of sharing food. For each of Jesus' disciples, there is some particular thing that they remember that makes them recognize Jesus, under all circumstances. There is more than one way of recognizing life – in fact, there may be a different way for every person, because life is so individual. Every child born is completely different, completely itself, so it might well follow that every person's new, resurrection life is as individual, as different. In which case, as each of us meets it in Jesus, it may take a while to recognize it.

Even when the disciples are together, so that they meet Jesus as a group and can reinforce each other's memories, both of Jesus himself and of the new life they had begun to glimpse together in being his followers, the life of Jesus is strange. They do recognize him as he comes to meet them in the Upper Room, where they often used to meet, and where they had shared the last meal with him before his crucifixion. Or when he cooks them breakfast on the shore of the lake, after they had been

fishing. Both the Upper Room and the lakeside are familiar
places, with lots of associations for the disciples of the happy
times with Jesus. In these places, he is much more recognizable.

But even here, the disciples cannot deceive themselves into
believing that they have Jesus back, just like old times, and that
now they can go on as though nothing has happened. Like Mary

in the garden, they have to learn that Jesus' life can no longer be contained. The crucifixion has changed everything. The old life has gone, and now the new life has come. The person they so loved and admired is both there and not there. He comes to them, but then he disappears again. He is no longer theirs.

That must have been so very hard for the disciples. They had lost him once, and just when they thought they had found him again, he changes. It is as though they are losing him all over again.

The hard, hard lesson that the disciples have to learn is that they can only have Jesus back if they share him. Every time they tell other people about Jesus, every time they do something that witnesses to their belief in life, they feel Jesus close again.

In *True Resurrection*, Harry Williams describes the resurrection like this:

> *If we have been aware of resurrection in this life, then, and only then, shall we be able or ready to receive the hopes of final resurrection after physical death. Resurrection as our final and ultimate future can be known only by those who perceive resurrection with us now encompassing all we are and do. For only then will it be recognised as a country we have already entered and in whose light and warmth we have already lived.*

That's why each person recognizes the risen Jesus differently. Each can only understand as much as they themselves have made room for, through their own awareness of life. Resurrection life is not different in kind from the life we all live, all of the time. All of it is, Christians believe, a gift from God. Belief in resurrection life is simply a blinding realization that God wants us to be alive enough to recognize divine life and share in it. Every time we trust in life, share life and rejoice in life, we are beginning the process that will enable us to recognize the undying life that we are all promised through the resurrection of Jesus.

So anything that rejoices in the mysterious, joyful life of the world will help us to start to celebrate Easter truth. Rejoicing in life, in all its variety and abundance, will help to prepare us to recognize God's new resurrection life.

Picture Acknowledgments

p.13 Pinturicchio (1454–1513): John the Baptist in the Desert. Siena, Cathedral © 1990, Photo Opera Metropolitana Siena/Scala, Florence.

p.15 Master of the Life of Mary (15th cent.): Polyptych with Scenes from the Life of Mary: Visitation. Munich, Alte Pinakothek © 1990, Photo Scala, Florence.

p.18 Cima da Conegliano (c. 1459–c. 1517): Baptism of Christ. Venice, Church of San Giovanni in Bragora © 2001, Photo Scala, Florence.

p.24 Peeters, Clara (1594–1659): Table with Cakes, Chicken and Olives. Madrid, Prado © 1994, Photo Scala, Florence.

p.27 Repin, Ilya (1844–1930): Temptation of Christ. Kiev, Russian Art State Museum © 1990, Photo Scala, Florence.

p.31 Tintoretto (1518–1594): Miracle of the Loaves and Fishes. Riverdale-on-Hudson, Moss Stanley Coll. © 1994, Photo Scala, Florence.

p.37 Reyneau, Betsy Graves (1888–1964): Portrait of Paul Robeson (as Othello), singer, actor, civil rights leader (1898–1976). Oil on canvas, 1943–44. (*Copyright). Washington DC, Natl. Portrait Gall., Smithsonian © 2004, Photo Nat. Portrait Gall. Smithsonian/Art Resource/Scala, Florence.

p.39 Rubens, Peter Paul (1577–1640): Supper in the House of the Pharisee. St. Petersburg, Hermitage Museum © 1990, Photo Scala, Florence.

p.41 Mafai, Mario (1902–1965): Landscape in Rome from the Pincio, 1937. Florence, Della Ragione Coll. © 1990, Photo Scala, Florence.

p.45 Giotto (1266–1336): Kiss of Judas. Padua, Scrovegni Chapel © 1990, Photo Scala, Florence.

p.48 Frith, William Powell (1819–1909): The Bridge of Love. London, Victoria and Albert Museum © 1990, Photo Scala, Florence.

p.54 Angelico, Fra (1387–1455): Christ Nailed to the Cross. Florence, Museo di San Marco © 1990, Photo Scala, Florence – courtesy of the Ministero Beni e Att. Culturali.

p.61 Giotto (1266–1336): Washing of the Feet. Padua, Scrovegni Chapel © 1990, Photo Scala, Florence.

p.62 Angelico, Fra (1387–1455): Silverware Cabinet – detail (Entry into Jerusalem). Florence, Museo di San Marco © 1990, Photo Scala, Florence – courtesy of the Ministero Beni e Att. Culturali.

p.65 Tarchiani, Filippo (17th cent.): Agony in the Garden. Florence, Museo di San Marco © 1990, Photo Scala, Florence – courtesy of the Ministero Beni e Att. Culturali.

p.66 Ghe, Nikolay (1831–1894): What is the Truth? (Christ before Pilate). Moscow, Tretyakov State Gallery © 1990, Photo Scala, Florence.

p.71 'Pray remember the blind'; scene under Covent Garden piazza, Cries of London, 1811. London, Guildhall Library & Art Gallery © 2003, Photo Scala Florence/HIP.

p.75 Stradano, Giovanni (1523–1605): Expulsion of the Merchants from the Temple. Florence, Santo Spirito © 1991, Photo Scala, Florence.

p.77 Gatti, Bernardino (1495–1575): Crucifixion. Parma, Palazzo Comunale © 1990, Photo Scala, Florence.

p.79 Gaddiano Manuscript 247. Florence, Biblioteca Laurenziana (Laurentian Library) © 1990, Photo Scala, Florence – courtesy of the Ministero Beni e Att. Culturali.

p.83 Duccio di Buoninsegna (c. 1260–1318): Maesta, back: Pilate Washing His Hands. Siena, Museo dell'Opera Metropolitana © 1990, Photo Opera Metropolitana Siena/Scala, Florence.

p.86 Valentin, Jean (1594–1632): The Denial of Peter. Moscow, Pushkin Museum © 1998, Photo Scala, Florence.

p.89 Greco, El (1541–1614): Tears of Saint Peter. Toledo, Hospital de Tavera © 1990, Photo Scala, Florence.

p.90 Dyck, Anthony van (1599–1641): Christ on the Cross. Naples, Museo di Capodimonte © 1990, Photo Scala, Florence – courtesy of the Ministero Beni e Att. Culturali.

p.94 Baegert, Derick the Elder (c. 1440–c. 1515): Altarpiece of the Passion – detail (Crucifixion). Munich, Alte Pinakothek © 1990, Photo Scala, Florence.

p.97 Munch, Edvard (1863–1944): The Sick Girl. Oslo, Nasjonalgalleriet © 1990, Photo Scala, Florence.

p.99 Goya, Francisco de (1746–1828): Crucifixion – detail (Christ's face). Madrid, Prado © 1990, Photo Scala, Florence.

p.102 Munch, Edvard (1863–1944): The Scream. Oslo, Nasjonalgalleriet © 1990, Photo Scala, Florence.

p.105 Savitzky, Konstantin (1841–1905): The Troop Train. St. Petersburg, Russian State Museum © 1990, Photo Scala, Florence.

p.106 Sebastiano del Piombo (c. 1485–1547): Flagellation. Rome, Church of San Pietro in Montorio © 1998, Photo Scala, Florence.

p.108 Schedoni, Bartolomeo (c. 1570–1615): The Deposition of Christ. Parma, Galleria Nazionale © 1993, Photo Scala, Florence – courtesy of the Ministero Beni e Att. Culturali.

p.113 Bruegel, Jan the Elder (1568–1625): Jesus Christ Releasing Souls from Limbo. The Hague, Mauritshuis © 1990, Photo Scala, Florence.

p.115 Schedoni, Bartolomeo (c. 1570–1615): The Three Marys at the Tomb. Parma, Galleria Nazionale © 1993, Photo Scala, Florence – courtesy of the Ministero Beni e Att. Culturali.

pp.118/119 Monet, Claude (1840–1926): The Garden of the Hoschede' Family at Montgeron. St. Petersburg, Hermitage Museum © 1990, Photo Scala, Florence.

p.122 Scarsellino, Ippolito (1551–1620): Christ and His Disciples on the Way to Emmaus. Rome, Galleria Borghese © 1990, Photo Scala, Florence – courtesy of the Minstero Beni e Att. Culturali.

p.124 Duccio di Buoninsegna (c. 1260–1318): Maesta, upper section: Appearance on the Sea of Galilee. Siena, Museo dell'Opera Metropolitana © 1990, Photo Opera Metropolitana Siena/Scala, Florence.